The Quotable Quote Book

The Quotable Quote Book

Merrit Malloy
and Shauna Sorensen

A CITADEL PRESS BOOK
Published by Carol Publishing Group

A Citadel Press Book
Published by Carol Publishing Group

Editorial Offices   Sales & Distribution Offices
600 Madison Avenue   120 Enterprise Avenue
New York, NY 10022   Secaucus, NJ 07094

In Canada: Musson Book Company
A division of General Publishing Co. Limited
Don Mills, Ontario

Manufactured in the United States of America
10 9 8 7 6 5 4 3 2 1

Library of Congress Cataloging-in-Publication Data

The Quotable quote book / compiled by Merrit Malloy and Shauna
    Sorensen.
        p. cm.
      ISBN 0-8065-1210-5 -- ISBN 0-8065-1220-2 (pbk.)
      1. Quotations, English. I. Malloy, Merrit. II. Sorensen,
    Shauna.
    PN6081.059   1990
    051–dc20   90-43763
                                                   CIP

This book is dedicated to the remarkable friendship
of women and especially to these three beloved allies,
Vanessa Bernacchi, Molly Malloy Wiest,
and O'Brian "Mac" Wiest,
who are also our daughters.

And to those cherished ones, who carried us, from
time to time, over rough terrain, a resounding
"Thank You" to
Dixie Bear
Grace Hodgson
Rosetta Sorensen
Helen Malloy
Carrie Alice Myers and
Bridget O'Donnell

Introduction

This book began as a private archive of wit, wisecracks and opinions. It was gathered from the "often wise and seldom quoted" among our friends and families, from the unheralded sages in our neighborhoods and on the job. It has now grown to include the famous, the infamous, and a broad cross-section of the current commentary of our time. In the early days of this compilation, we referred to this collection as *The Philosophers of the Late 20th Century,* which is what it has essentially remained. The only "current" quote book available, it is a veritable Berlitz course in modern thinking.

With all due respect to the genius of Shakespeare, Voltaire, Goethe, Plato, Descartes et al., we humbly present here the commentary of the latter part of the 20th century, which is often similar in spirit, yet distinct, unique to its time, a lot funnier and easier to understand.

We live in an era of the greatest dissemination and exchange of ideas and information in known history. From this broad and prolific base, here then are some of the voices currently being heard.

Merrit Malloy and Shauna Sorensen
Summer, 1990

Please note. All known sources of quotes are duly noted in the Index Notes at the end of the book.

Contents

Achievement

Success follows doing what you want to do. There is no other way to be successful.

Malcolm Forbes

She didn't know it couldn't be done so she went ahead and did it.

Mary's Almanac

What one has to do usually can be done.

Anna Eleanor Roosevelt

Those who dare to fail miserably can achieve greatly.

Robert F. Kennedy

Acting

Acting is making it seem like it's happening now.

Anne Jackson

Some of the greatest love affairs I've ever known involved one actor — unassisted.

Wilson Mizner

Just show up. Be there.

Jack Albertson

Disney, of course, has the best casting. If he doesn't like an actor, he just tears him up.

Alfred Hitchcock

Harold, don't sleep like a great man. Just sleep.

Stella Adler to
Harold Clurman

Work for reality, not approval.

Eric Morris

Actors die so loud.

Henry Miller

Just learn your lines and don't bump into the furniture.

Spencer Tracy

I'm no actor. And I have sixty-four pictures to prove it.

Victor Mature

The actor is not quite a human being—but then, who is?

George Sanders

I used to go out with actresses and other female impersonators.

Mort Sahl

I have to act to live.

Sir Laurence Olivier

Do your job and demand your compensation—but in that order.

Cary Grant

First Rule of Acting: Whatever happens, look as if it were intended.

Arthur Bloch

Attempt the impossible in order to improve your work.

Bette Davis

LIVE! I can't go on LIVE!! I'm a movie star—not an actor!

Peter O'Toole, in *My Favorite Year*

I don't like showing the technique. I don't like people who say, "Here, I'm going to act, but first I have to bounce off this wall." If you have to bounce off the wall, do it by yourself. Don't feature the technique. My old drama coach used to say, "Don't just do something, stand there." Gary Cooper wasn't afraid to do nothing.

Clint Eastwood

It can be a simple sentence that makes one simple point, and you build from that. You zero in on the one moment that gets that character: you go for it. That's it man, and if you fail, the whole thing is down the drain, but if you make it, you hit the moon.

Jack Lemmon

Don't get married to an actress, because they're also actresses in bed.

Roberto Rossellini

A lot of what acting is is paying attention.

Robert Redford

Don't use your conscious past. Use your creative imagination to create a past that belongs to your characters.

Stella Adler

Never let them see you sweat.

Actor Axiom

It's such a cuckoo business. And it's a business you go into because you are egocentric. It's a very embarrassing profession.

Katharine Hepburn

It's not true that I said "actors are cattle." I said "they should be treated like cattle."

Alfred Hitchcock

(Acting) is an extension of life. How you're capable of performing in your life, that's how you're capable of performing on screen.

John Cassavetes

Acting is a matter of giving away secrets.

Ellen Barkin

I believe you can't be an actor if you haven't had the feeling of being abandoned as a child.

Isabelle Adjani

An actor is a guy who, if you ain't talking about him, ain't listening.

Marlon Brando

Joan of Arc should be played as a "pain in the ass" and how do I know she was a "pain in the ass"? . . . because they burn her at the end.

Harold Clurman

Action

Just do it.

Ad for NIKE

Action is the only reality, not only reality but morality as well.

Abbie Hoffman

The only measure of what you believe is what you do. If you want to know what people believe, don't read what they write, don't ask them what they believe, just observe what they do.

Ashley Montagu, Ph.D.

The only way to get positive feelings about yourself is to take positive actions. Man does not live as he thinks, he thinks as he lives.

Reverend Vaughan Quinn, O.M.I.

Inaction may be the biggest form of action.

Jerry Brown

Action based only on principles isn't always good even if it feels good.

John Chancellor

Love is a verb.

Sister Mary Tricky

Advice

Never sleep with anybody who has more problems than you do.

> Robert McKee

Ride the horse in the direction that it's going.

> Werner Erhard

If it's not working, plug it in.

> Sears Repairman

They aren't kidding when they say, "Wash Whites separately."

> Wes Smith

Never trust a naked busdriver.

> Jack Douglas

Never go to a doctor whose office plants are dead.

> Erma Bombeck

Dare to be cute.

> George Lucas

Always take an extra quarter to the laundry room.

Wes Smith

Don't accept rides from strange men, and remember that all men are strange.

Robin Morgan

I have a simple philosophy. Fill what's empty. Empty what's full. Scratch where it itches.

Alice Roosevelt Longworth

Never eat more than you can lift.

Miss Piggy

Never accept a drink from a urologist.

Erma Bombeck's father

Keep breathing.

Sophie Tucker

Never go to bed mad. Stay up and fight.

Phyllis Diller

Do not marry the enemy of your excitement.

Nathaniel Branden

Never lend your car to anyone to whom you have given birth.

Erma Bombeck

Start slow and taper off.

Walt Stack

A woman in love will do almost anything for a man, except give up the desire to improve him.

Nathaniel Branden

Never give a party if you will be the most interesting person there.

Mickey Friedman

Be straightforward in the way you dodge issues.

Anonymous

You should treat all disasters as if they were trivialities but never treat a triviality as if it were a disaster.

Quentin Crisp

Better a tooth out than always aching.

Thomas Fuller

When you can't solve the problem, manage it.

Robert H. Schuller

Seize the day!

Motto, *Dead Poets Society*

You're never too old to do goofy stuff.

Ward Cleaver, "Leave It to Beaver"

Always enter a strange hotel room with extreme caution, especially one with a samurai warrior in it.

> Thomas Magnum, "Magnum, P.I."

When things go wrong, don't go with them.

> Anonymous

Begin somewhere; you cannot build a reputation on what you intend to do.

> Liz Smith

Don't accept that others know you better than you know yourself.

> Dr. Sonja Friedman

As a Grandfather, I'm entitled to a few words of sage advice to the young:

I would spend more time with my children.

I would make my money before spending it.

I would learn the joys of wine instead of hard liquor.

I would not smoke cigarettes when I had pneumonia.

I would not marry a fifth time.

> John Huston

You can lead a herring to water, but you have to walk really fast or they die.

> Rose Nylund, "The Golden Girls"

Never floss a stranger.

> Joan Rivers

The only way to convert a heathen is to travel into the jungle.

> Lane Kirkland (on working with capitalists)

Go to bed. What you're staying up for isn't worth it.

> Andy Rooney

Never look down on anybody unless you're helping them up.

> Rev. Jesse Jackson

Think of a big color—who cares if people call you Rothko. Release your childhood. Release it.

> Larry Rivers & Frank O'Hara

Good advice is one of those insults that ought to be forgiven.

> Anonymous

Bloom where you are planted.

> N.R. Campion's Aunt Grace

If it's working, keep doing it.
If it's not working, stop doing it.
If you don't know what to do, don't do anything.

> Medical School advice given to
> Dr. Melvin Konner

The best way to survive an accident is not to get into one.

Ad for Subaru

Photographer's advice: Stand in the right place.
David Douglas Duncan

Follow your bliss.

Joseph Campbell

Above all, do not talk yourself out of good ideas by trying to expound them at haphazard meetings.
Jacques Barzun

Whatever you do, don't smoke.

Yul Brynner
(just before he died of lung cancer)

Flush.

Robert Fulghum

Never call anybody an asshole. It hardly ever works.
Marilyn Peterson

Don't worry about growing older or pleasing others. Please yourself.

David Brown

If you don't like something about yourself, change it. If you can't change it, accept it.
Ted Shackelford

Aging

By the time we've made it, we've had it.

Malcolm Forbes

Old people shouldn't eat health foods. They need all the preservatives they can get.

Robert Orben

I don't worry about getting old. I'm old already. Only young people worry about getting old. When I was 65, I had Cupid's eczema. I don't believe in dying. It's been done. I'm working on a new exit. Besides, I can't die now—I'm booked.

George Burns

One of the chief pleasures of middle age is looking back at the people you didn't marry.

'70s Anonymous

You can't help getting older but you don't have to get old.

George Burns

The secret of staying young is to live honestly, eat slowly, and lie about your age.

Lucille Ball

Just remember, once you're over the hill you begin to pick up speed.

Charles Schultz

The hardest years in life are those between ten and seventy.

Helen Hayes (at 73)

Don't worry about avoiding temptation. As you grow older, it will avoid you.

Joey Adams

Now that I'm over sixty, I'm veering toward respectability.

Shelley Winters

Contrary to popular belief, as your body ages, it's not the knees that go first.

Ad for Foltene

My Mother always used to say: "The older you get, the better you get—unless you're a banana."

Rose Nylund, "The Golden Girls"

Acceptance is the word we must substitute for dependence in dealing with the aged. Their acceptance of help, ours of their need.

Maureen Howard

If a thing is old, it is a sign that it was fit to live. The guarantee of continuity is quality.

Eddie Rickenbacker

America

(America) is the only country in the world where failing to promote yourself is regarded as being arrogant.

Garry Trudeau

There's three moments in a man's life: when he buys a house, a car, and a new color TV. That's what America is all about.

Archie Bunker, "All in the Family"

Land of my dreams—Home of the Whopper.

Balki Bartokomous, "Perfect Strangers"

If you speak three languages, you are trilingual. If you speak two languages, you are bilingual. If you speak one language, you're American.

Sonny Spoon

As Miss America, my goal is to bring peace to the entire world and then to get my own apartment.

Jay Leno

We take hamburgers more seriously than anyone else.

Ray Kroc, founder of McDonald's

If American men are obsessed with money, American women are obsessed with weight. The men talk of gain, the women of loss, and I do not know which talk is the more boring.

Marya Mannes

Suburbia is where the developer bulldozes out the trees, then names the streets after them.

Bill Vaughn

Americans are a broad minded people. They'll accept the fact that a person can be an alcoholic, a dope fiend, a wife beater, and even a newspaperman, but if a man doesn't drive there's something wrong with him.

Art Buchwald

There's so much plastic in this culture that vinyl leopard skin is becoming an endangered synthetic.

Lily Tomlin

In America sex is an obsession, in other parts of the world it is a fact.

Marlene Dietrich

Goodnight America—wherever you are.

Jack Killian, "Midnight Caller"

18

What vegetable would your husband most like to sit on?
Bob Eubanks, "The Newlywed Game"

Anger

I'm mad as hell and I'm not going to take it anymore!
Howard Beall, *Network*

Cameron's so tight if you stick a piece of coal up his ass
in two weeks you'll have a diamond.
Ferris Bueller, *Ferris
Bueller's Day Off*

Anger is a lot like a piece of shredded wheat caught
under your dentures. If you leave it there you'll get a
blister and you gotta eat Jell-O all week. If you get rid
of it, the sore heals and you feel better.
Sophia Petrillo, "The Golden Girls"

The only one you get even with is yourself.
Bob Mandel

The angry people are those people who are most afraid.
Dr. Robert Anthony

Animals

There is something going on now in Mexico that I happen to think is cruelty to animals. What I'm talking about, of course, is cat juggling.

Steve Martin

One thing for sure — a sheep is not a creature of the air.

Graham Chapman, "Monty Python's
Flying Circus"

Never send a man to do a horse's job.

Mr. Ed, "Mr. Ed"

Due to the shape of the North American elk's esophagus even if it could speak, it could not pronounce the word lasagna.

Cliff Clavin, "Cheers"

Art

First I have a think, and then I put a line around it.

Roger Fry

It's either easy or impossible.

Salvador Dali

An artist is always out of step with his time. He has to be.

The New York Times

Art is only a means to life, the life more abundant. It merely points the way.

Henry Miller

When a piece gets difficult, make faces.

Vladimir Horowitz

A lotta cats copy the Mona Lisa, but people still line up to see the original.

Louis "Satchmo" Armstrong

When she was here, the place was magical. Now it's just three funny buildings.

> Diana Mackeon on Louise Nevelson

I don't want people who want to dance, I want people who have to dance.

> George Balanchine

An artist is somebody who produces things that people don't need to have.

> Andy Warhol

If it weren't for art, there wouldn't be any science.

> Penny Robinson, "Lost in Space"

I don't think it's very useful to open wide the door for young artists; the ones who break down the door are much more interesting.

> Paul Schrader

I am only a public entertainer who has understood his time.

> Pablo Picasso

I could have told you Vincent, the world it was not made for one as beautiful as you.

> Song lyric, "Vincent," Don McLean
> (written for Vincent Van Gogh)

Awards

You like me. You really like me!
  Sally Fields, on receiving her Oscar for Best Actress

This medal (the National Book Award) together with my American Express card, will identify me worldwide . . . except at Bloomingdale's.
  S.J. Perelman

Peanut prizes inspire monkey contestants.
  Unknown

Beauty

I'm tired of all this nonsense about beauty being only skin-deep. That's deep enough. What do you want, an adorable pancreas?

Jean Kerr

You'd be surprised how much it costs to look this cheap.

Dolly Parton

Beauty comes in all sizes — not just size 5.

Roseanne Barr

She got her good looks from her father. He's a plastic surgeon.

Groucho Marx

You are so beautiful to me.

Song lyric, "You Are So Beautiful," sung by Joe Cocker

Behavior

The key point about a demonstration is that it must be seen. Hence the term "demonstration." If a person demonstrates privately in his own home, this is not technically a demonstration but merely "acting silly" or "behaving like an ass."

Woody Allen

A woman marries hoping he will change but he doesn't; a man marries a woman hoping she won't change and she does.

Recent Adage

There are very few people who don't become more interesting when they stop talking.

Mary Lowry

In short, the best thing to do is behave in a manner befitting one's age. If you are sixteen or under, try not to go bald.

Woody Allen

We got new advice as to what motivated man to walk upright: to free his hands for masturbation.

Jane Wagner

She entered a room as though she were slicing it in half with a knife.

Walter Kerr of
Bette Davis

Boredom, like necessity, is very often the mother of invention.

Dr. Smith, "Lost in Space"

I don't say we all ought to misbehave, but we ought to look as if we could.

Orson Welles

It's by what you do that you communicate to others that you are deeply involved in their well being.

Ashley Montagu, Ph.D.

Birth

Having a baby is like taking your lower lip and forcing it over your head.

Carol Burnett

There are no illegitimate babies.

Merrit Malloy

If pregnancy were a book, they would cut the last two chapters.

Nora Ephron

I've laid several eggs, but only two have been fertilized.

Ernestyne White

Somewhere on this globe every ten seconds, there is a woman giving birth to a child. She must be found and stopped.

Sam Levinson

The Body

I see your schwartz is as big as mine. Now let's see how
well you handle it.

> Rick Moranis to Bill Pullman,
> *Spaceballs*

Be true to your teeth and they won't be false to you.

> Soupy Sales

The human body contains 206 bones; women do not
have one more rib than men.

> Claudia Bowe

Bumper Stickers

You're only young once . . . ONCE!

If you can read this, you're too damn close.

Honk, if you love Jesus.

Honk, if you're horny.

If a mother's place is in the home, how come I spend so
  much time in the car?

Nature bats last.

I brake for insights.

Lotus Weinstock

Accountants work their assets off.

A woman's place is in the mall.

Use your voice, vote for choice.

If I have to explain, you wouldn't understand.

Harley Davidson Co.

Turn it over.

No left turn unstoned.

It's never to late to have a happy childhood.

Dream the bison back.

Business

Business is a good game—lots of competition and a minimum of rules. You keep score with money.

> Nolan Bushnell,
> Atari founder

Some people find oil. Others don't.

> J. Paul Getty

Your business is to put me out of business.

> Dwight D. Eisenhower

Both business and love require the temperament of a vampire combined with the discretion of an anemone.

> Steiner

Few great men could pass Personnel.

> Paul Goodman

Greed is good! Greed is right! Greed works! Greed will save the U.S.A.!

> Michael Douglas, *Wall Street*

Wives of corporate executives who babble indiscreetly at lunch are a rich source of financial information. Listen carefully and buy them another drink.

David Brown

You know what makes this country great? You don't have to be witty or clever, as long as you can hire someone who is.

Ted Baxter, "The Mary Tyler Moore Show"

Opportunity can't knock unless it's on your doorstep.

The Wall Street Journal

Start planning your second career while you're still on your first one.

David Brown

You can't wait for the phone to ring. You have to ring them.

Lord Lew Grade

Always live better than your clients, so that they won't object to the fees you demand.

Ben Sonnenberg

You can't make one thin dime giving people what they need. You've got to give 'em what they want.

Angel Martin, "The Rockford Files"

To sell something you have to someone who wants it—
that is not business. But to sell something you don't
have to someone who doesn't want it—that's business.

From *The Big Book of Jewish Humor*

We make money the old-fashioned way—we earn it.

Ad for Smith-Barney

We make money the old-fashioned way—we borrow it.

Stockbroker, "Barney Miller"

Comedy may be big business, but it isn't pretty.

Steve Martin

Putting you first made us #1.

Ad for General Motors

Did you ever hear of a kid playing accountant—even if
he wanted to be one?

Jackie Mason

Progress might have been right once, but it's gone on
too long.

Ogden Nash

Bureaucracy

We don't care. We don't have to. We're the phone company.

> Lily Tomlin as Ernestine,
> "Laugh-In"

Sex in the hands of public educators is not a pretty thing.

> Kevin Arnold, "The Wonder Years"

People who claw their way to the top are not likely to find very much wrong with the system that enabled them to rise.

> Arthur Schlesinger, Jr.

California

The west coast of Iowa.

Joan Didion

It's a scientific fact that if you stay in California, you lose one point of IQ every year.

Truman Capote

A wet dream in the mind of New York.

Erica Jong

California is a tragic country, like Palestine, like every promised land.

Christopher Isherwood

The more someone dislikes California, the more likely he or she is from an eastern state. The more extreme the dislike, the more likely he or she is from Ohio.

E. Garrison

It never rains in Southern California,
It pours, baby, it pours.

Song lyric, "It Never Rains in Southern California"

Capital Punishment

Murder is the execution of someone that the murderer thinks is guilty and execution is the murder of someone society thinks is guilty.

John Riley

It's a proven fact that capital punishment is a known detergent against crime.

Archie Bunker, "All in the Family"

Catholics

Catholicism has changed tremendously in recent years. Now when Communion is served there is also a salad bar.

Bill Marr

Where I come from, when a Catholic marries a Lutheran it is considered the first step on the road to Minneapolis.

Garrison Keillor

Cats

Love to eat those mousies, mousies what I love to eat.

Kliban

Cats are intended to teach us that not everything in nature has a purpose.

Garrison Keillor

Dogs come when they're called; cats take a message and get back to you.

Mary Bly

The only good cat is a stir-fried cat.

"Alf"

Character

We are born princes and the civilizing process makes us frogs.

Eric Berne

Some men are born mediocre, some men achieve mediocrity, and some men have mediocrity thrust upon them.

Joseph Heller

Being generous is inborn; being altruistic is a learned perversity.

Robert Heinlein

Idealism is fine, but as it approaches reality the cost becomes prohibitive.

William F. Buckley

An ounce of hypocrisy is worth a pound of ambition.

Michael Korda

Woe to him inside a non-conformist clique who does not conform to non-conformity.

Eric Hoffer

Beware of altruism. It is based on self-deception, the root of all evil.

Robert Heinlein

A fanatic is a man who redoubles his efforts after he has forgotten his aims.

George Santayana

It's a rare person who wants to hear what he doesn't want to hear.

Dick Cavett

To gain that which is worth having, it may be necessary to lose everything else.

Bernadette Devlin

We can tell our values by looking at our checkbook stubs.

Gloria Steinem

A gentleman is a man who can play the accordian but doesn't.

Anonymous

Irresponsibility isn't a sickness — it's an art.
Remington Steele, "Remington Steele"

Champions take responsibility. When the ball is coming over the net, you can be sure I want the ball.

Billie Jean King

Keep in mind that the true meaning of an individual is how he treats a person who can do him absolutely no good.

Ann Landers

I cannot believe that the purpose of life is to be "happy." I think the purpose of life is to be useful, to be responsible, to be honorable, to be compassionate. It is, after all, to matter: to count, to stand for something, to have made some difference that you lived at all.

Leo C. Rosten

A human being has no discernible character until he acts.

Constantine Nash & Virginia Oakley

Children

Dear Mom and Dad, Leave $50,000 in a bag under the bridge on Decatur Street. If there is no bridge on Decatur Street, please build one.

Woody Allen

We are given children to test us and make us more spiritual.

George Will

Children make the most desirable opponents in Scrabble as they are both easy to beat and fun to cheat.

Fran Lebowitz

My children weary me. I can only see them as defective adults: feckless, destructive, frivolous, sensual, humorless.

Evelyn Waugh

God bless the child who's got his own.

Song lyric, "God Bless the Child,"
Billie Holiday

They should be neither seen nor heard and no one should make another one.

Gore Vidal

If you've never been hated by your child, you have never been a parent.

Bette Davis

I hate babies. They're so human.

H.H. Munro

Never raise your hand to your children—it leaves your midsection unprotected.

Robert Orben

Never have children, only grandchildren.

Gore Vidal

I can't believe I forgot to have children.

'80s Anonymous saying

To teenagers: Straighten up your room first, then the world.

Jeff Jordan

Your children need your presence more than your presents.

Rev. Jesse Jackson

There are only two lasting bequests we can hope to give our children. One of these is roots, the other wings.

Hodding Carter

The thing about having a baby is that thereafter you have it.

Jean Kerr

By giving children lots of affection, you can help fill them with love and acceptance of themselves. Then that's what they will have to give away.

Dr. Wayne Dyer

When I was a kid my parents moved alot — but I always found them.

Rodney Dangerfield

We are the world. We are the children.

Song lyric, "We Are the World,"
Lionel Ritchie and Michael Jackson

Choices

There are two ways of meeting difficulties. You alter the difficulties or you alter yourself to meet them.

Phyliss Bottome

You gotta play the hand that's dealt you. There may be pain in that hand, but you play it. And I've played it.

James Brady, Presidential Press
Secretary

Don't let other people tell you what you want.

Pat Riley

Pick battles big enough to matter, small enough to win.

Jonathan Kozel

Look for your choices, pick the best one, then go with it.

Pat Riley

In not making the decision, you've made one. Not doing something is the same as doing it.

Ivan Bloch

Commitment

With regard to ham and eggs: The chicken is involved; the pig is committed.

Anonymous '80s Axiom

What you can't get out of, get into wholeheartedly.

Mignon McLaughlin

47

Common Sense

If you want to catch trout, don't fish in a herring barrel.

Ann Landers

Never buy a fur from a vegetarian.

Joan Rivers

If you don't throw it, they can't hit it.

Lefty Gomez

You don't thank a terrorist for improving airline security.

Federal Prosecutor Ellen Meltzer

There is so little difference between husbands, you might as well keep the first.

Adela Rogers St. John

Communication

What you can't communicate runs your life.

Dr. Robert Anthony

Many are called. But few are called back.

Sister Mary Tricky

I wish people who have trouble communicating would just shut up.

Tom Lehrer

Don't look over people's shoulders. Look in their eyes. Don't talk at your children. Take their faces in your hands and talk to them. Don't make love to a body, make love to a person.

Leo Buscaglia

Asking is just polite demanding.

"Max Headroom"

The opposite of talking isn't listening. The opposite of talking is waiting.

Fran Liebowitz

Talk about a dream, try to make it real.

>> Song lyric, "Badlands," sung by
>> Bruce Springsteen

Don't say it—spray it.

>> Graffiti Slogan

Talk low, talk slow, and don't say too much.

>> John Wayne

The difference between news and gossip lies in whether you raise your voice or lower it.

>> Franklin P. Jones

In Maine we have a saying that there's no point in speaking unless you can improve on silence.

>> Edmund Muskie

Have I reached the person to whom I am speaking?

>> Lily Tomlin as "Ernestine"

The best impromptu speeches are those written well in advance.

>> Ruth Gordon

What you said is exactly what you intended to say.

>> Dr. Robert Anthony

Compassion

If we are not our brother's keeper, let us at least not be his executioner.

Marlon Brando

Don't be a noble fighter, " 'cause kindness is righter."

Popeye

Keep the other person's well-being in mind when you feel an attack of soul-purging truth coming on.

Betty White

We live very close together. So, our prime purpose in this life is to help others. And if you can't help them, at least don't hurt them.

The Dalai Lama

Country

There's a little country in all of us, a little frontier.
> Louis L'Amour

Mama, don't let your babies grow up to be cowboys.
> Song lyric, Patsy and Ed Bruce

Courage

Living at risk is jumping off the cliff and building your wings on the way down.

Ray Bradbury

Never stop. One always stops as soon as something is about to happen.

Peter Brook

You must do the thing you think you cannot do.

Eleanor Roosevelt

Never confuse a single defeat with a final defeat.

F. Scott Fitzgerald

Everyone has talent. What is rare is the courage to follow the talent to the dark place where it leads.

Erica Jong

A coward dies a hundred deaths, a brave man only once . . . But then, once is enough, isn't it?

Judge Harry Stone, "Night Court"

Wanna do something outrageous? Come to my house and say to my mother-in-law, "You're wrong, fatso!"

Buddy Sorrell, "The Dick Van Dyke Show"

By not coming forward (about rape), you make yourself a victim forever.

Kelly McGillis, *People* Magazine

Courage is doing what you are afraid to do. There can be no courage unless you're scared.

Eddie Rickenbacker

It is very easy to forgive others their mistakes. It takes more guts and gumption to forgive them for having witnessed your own.

Jessamyn West

Creativity

Don't think! Thinking is the enemy of creativity. It's self-conscious, and anything self-conscious is lousy. You can't try to do things; you simply must do them.

Ray Bradbury

The very essence of the creative is its novelty, and hence we have no standard by which to judge it.

Carl Rogers

Artists die twice. First creatively. Then physically. The second one is the easiest.

Sylvester Stallone

Critics

Any reviewer who expresses rage and loathing for a novel is preposterous. He or she is like a person who has put on full armor and attacked a hot fudge sundae.

Kurt Vonnegut

Critics are like pigs at the pastry cart.

John Updike

Critics are like eunuchs in a harem. They're there every night, they see it done every night, they see how it should be done every night, but they can't do it themselves.

Brendan Behan

A critic is a man who creates nothing and thereby feels qualified to judge the work of creative men. There is logic in this; he is unbiased—he hates all creative people equally.

Robert Heinlein

A critic is someone who never actually goes to the battle yet who afterwards comes out shooting the wounded.

Tyne Daly

A critic is a man who knows the way but can't drive the car.

Kenneth Tynan

Cynicism

Cynicism is an unpleasant way of saying the truth.
Lillian Hellman

I worry no matter how cynical you become, it's never enough to keep up.

Jane Wagner

The worst cynicism: a belief of luck.
Joyce Carol Oates

Gossip is the opiate of the oppressed.

Erica Jong

Never accept an invitation from a stranger unless he offers you candy.

Linda Festa

Nobody loves me like my mother and she could be jivin' too.

B.B. King

There's nothing like a hardship song to set my toes a-tappin.

Roseanne Barr

Forgive your enemies, but never forget their names.

Ed Koch, Quoting John F. Kennedy

Moonlight is romantic, but it's hell to read by.

Remington Steele, "Remington Steele"

One of the advantages of living alone is that you don't have to wake up in the arms of a loved one.

Marion Smith

Death

It's not that I'm afraid to die. I just don't want to be there when it happens.

Woody Allen

For three days after death, hair and fingernails continue to grow but phone calls taper off.

Johnny Carson

Death is a distant rumor to the young.

Andy Rooney

There will be sex after death; we just won't be able to feel it.

Jane Wagner

Death ends a life. But it doesn't end a relationship.

Hal Holbrook, in
I Never Sang for My Father

Well, Norton, I guess they'll be no bus rides for me. I've come to the end of the line. I'm going to that big bus depot in the sky. It's a one-way trip with no transfers.

Ralph Kramden, "The Honeymooners"

Life is a series of bad jokes, and death tops them all.

A Dinner Guest, "The Saint"

There has never been such a silence.

Elizabeth Taylor, in *Cleopatra*

Like women all over America, my mother confronted tragedy and death with cold ham and Jell-O salad.

Kevin Arnold, "The Wonder Years"

Death is just nature's way of telling you, "Hey, you're not alive anymore."

Bull, "Night Court"

Martin Levine has passed away at the age of seventy-five. Mr. Levine had owned a movie theater chain here in New York. The funeral will be held on Tuesday, at 2:15, 4:20, 6:30, 8:40, and 10:50.

David Letterman

Always go to other people's funerals, otherwise they won't come to yours.

Yogi Berra

I postpone death by living, by suffering, by error, by risking, by giving, by losing.

Anais Nin

Death is like sleep without the long term commitment.

Comic Lea Krinsky

Death may not be funny, but it's not the end of the world.

Bud Blitzer

It's not the end of the physical body that should worry us. Rather our concern must be to live while we're alive.

Elizabeth Kubler-Ross

Defeat

Defeat is worse than death because you have to live with defeat.

Bill Musselman

The important thing is to learn a lesson every time you lose.

John McEnroe

You may be disappointed if you fail, but you are doomed if you don't try.

Beverly Sills

Delusion

Elderly customers think they are fifteen years younger than they actually are.

T. Lux Frances

Our ability to delude ourselves may be an important survival tool.

Jane Wagner

You're obviously suffering from delusions of adequacy.

Alexis Carrington, "Dynasty"

Diet

I have gained and lost the same ten pounds so many times over and over again my cellulite must have déjà vu.

Jane Wagner

The best way to lose weight is to get the flu and take a trip to Egypt.

Roz Lawrence

No diet will remove all the fat from your body because the brain is entirely fat. Without a brain you might look good, but all you could do is run for public office.

Covert Bailey

It's not what you're eating, it's what's eating you.

Dr. Janet Greeson

The first thing I remember liking that liked me back was food.

Rhoda Morgenstern, "Rhoda"

Why am I bothering to eat this chocolate? I might as well just apply it directly to my thighs.

Rhoda Morgenstern, "Mary Tyler Moore Show"

I'm so neurotic that I worry I'll lose weight when I'm on a diet.

Grace Hodgson

Divorce

I swear, if you existed, I'd divorce you.

> Elizabeth Taylor, *Who's Afraid
> of Virginia Woolf?*

Did you ever stop to think that paying alimony is like keeping up the payments on a car with four flats?

> "Laugh-In"

Judges, as a class, display, in the matter of arranging alimony, that reckless generosity which is found only in men who are giving away someone else's cash.

> P.G. Wodehouse

Hollywood is the only place in the world where an amicable divorce means each one getting fifty percent of the publicity.

> Lauren Bacall

Drugs & Alcohol

Mike Hammer drinks beer and not cognac because I can't spell cognac.

Mickey Spillane

A cap of good acid costs five dollars and for that you can hear the Universal symphony with God singing solo and the Holy Ghost on drums.

Hunter Thompson

Cocaine isn't habit forming and I know because I've been taking it for years.

Tallulah Bankhead

I envy people who drink—at least they know what to blame everything on.

Oscar Levant

I only drink to make other people seem interesting.

George Jean Nathan

I hate to advocate drugs, alcohol, violence, or insanity to anyone, but they've always worked for me.

Hunter Thompson

A productive drunk is the bane of moralists.

Unknown

If God wanted us high, He would have given us wings.

Arsenio Hall

On the highway, beware of rolling stoned.

Anonymous

If you drink, don't drive. Don't even putt.

Dean Martin

Drinking and driving can kill a friendship.

National Ad Council

Just say no.

Official anti-drug slogan

Sometimes I think it's a shame when I get feelin' better when I'm feelin' no pain.

Song lyric, Gordon Lightfoot

When you take speed, you're still going nowhere, only faster.

A Recovering Addict

The Economy

Economists are people who work with numbers but who don't have the personality to be accountants.

Unknown

Since nostaglia is fueled by inflation, could it be that inflation is the result of a conspiracy by the people who are trying to palm off McGovern buttons and Howdy Doody puppets and their Aunt Thelma's toaster as antiques.

Calvin Trillin

A study of economics usually reveals that the best time to buy anything is last year.

Marty Allen

I wonder what purpose junk mail has in the grand scheme of things?

Chris Cagney, "Cagney & Lacey"

In economics the majority is always wrong.

John Kenneth Galbraith

I learned more about the economy from one South Dakota dust storm than I did in all my years at college.

Hubert Humphrey

Expenditure rises to meet income.

C. Northcote Parkinson

Education

I think the world is run by C-students.

Al McGuire

University politics are so vicious precisely because the stakes are so small.

Henry Kissinger

Good teaching is one-fourth preparation and three-fourths theatre.

Gail Goodwin

If you think education is expensive, try ignorance.

Derek Bok

Nowadays, the illiterates can read and write.

Alberto Moravia

Studying literature at Harvard is like learning about women at the Mayo Clinic.

Ray Blount, Jr.

Next week I have to take my college aptitude test. In my high school they didn't even teach aptitude.

Tony Banta, "Taxi"

From your parents you learn love and laughter and how to put one foot in front of the other. But when books are opened you discover that you have wings.

Helen Hayes

The schools I went to as a kid made me wary. It was clear to me that everything was a lie except math.

Susan Shown Harjo, American Indian

One out of every five Americans is unable to read this sentence.

Ad for General Dynamics

I quit school in the fifth grade because of pneumonia. Not because I had it but because I couldn't spell it.

Rocky Graziano

Ego

Listen, everyone is entitled to my opinion.

Madonna

A team effort is a lot of people doing what I say.

Michael Winner,
British Film Director

A narcissist is someone better than you are.

Gore Vidal

A lot of people may not know this but I'm quite famous.

Sam Malone, "Cheers"

I would live in a communist country providing I was the Queen.

Stella Adler

If only I had a little humility, I'd be perfect.

Ted Turner

The great ones are never understood in their own life-times.

"Slap Maxwell"

My definition of a narcissist is a person who is having a great big love affair with himself, but he can't stand the object of his affections.

Reverend Vaughan Quinn

A lot of people say Jerry Lee Lewis done wrong, but that has yet to be proven in the eyes of God.

Jerry Lee Lewis

Arrogant, pompous, obnoxious, vain, cruel, persecuting, distasteful, verbose, a show-off. I have been called all of these. Of course, I am.

Howard Cosell

Coyness is a rather comically pathetic fault, a miscalculation in which, by trying to veil the ego, we let it appear stark naked.

Louis Kronenberger

Whenever I play, it should be an event. I'm a legend and I should keep it that way.

Little Richard

Ego is to the true self what a flashlight is to a spotlight.

John Bradshaw

The English

The English instinctively admire any man who has no talent and is modest about it.

James Agate

The English think incompetence is the same thing as sincerity.

Quentin Crisp

I didn't know he was dead; I thought he was British.

Unknown

Boy, the things I do for England.

Prince Charles
on sampling snake meat

I am the last of Britain's stately homos.

Quentin Crisp

I'm in favor of liberalized immigration because of the effect it would have on restaurants. I'd let just about everybody in except the English.

Calvin Trillin

The first thing you do when you're being stalked by an angry mob with raspberries is to release a tiger.

John Clease, "Monty Python"

Enlightenment

I'm astounded by people who want to "know" the universe when it's hard enough to find your way around Chinatown.

Woody Allen

Either this man is dead or my watch has stopped.

Groucho Marx

I know the answer! The answer lies within the heart of all mankind! The answer is twelve? I think I'm in the wrong building.

Charles Schultz

The secret of patience . . . to do something else in the meantime.

Anonymous

The game is not about becoming somebody, it's about becoming nobody.

Baba Ram Dass

No man is great enough or wise enough for any of us to surrender our destiny to. The only way in which anyone can lead us is to restore to us the belief in our own guidance.

Henry Miller

We have to move from the illusion of certainty to the certainty of illusion.

Sam Keen

Environment

Earth is a family business.

Bob Mandel

The universe is like a safe to which there is a combination. But the combination is locked up in the safe.

Peter DeVries

Nobody makes a greater mistake than he who did nothing because he could only do a little.

Edmund Burke

Energy efficiency is about getting the same, or better, services from less energy by substituting ingenuity for brute force.

Christopher Flavin and Alan B. Durning

Ethics

Either the right to live and die are both sacred, or neither is.

> Treska Lindsey

Do the right thing.

> Spike Lee

Your luck is how you treat people.

> Bridget O'Donnell

Ethics is about what is right, not who is right.

> Anonymous

Grub first, then ethics.

> Bertolt Brecht

What we might consider is how we are good rather
than how good we are.

> Merrit Malloy

Etiquette

If I had time to clean up the mess, I'd shoot you.

J.R. Ewing, "Dallas"

There are times not to flirt. When you're sick. When you're with children. When you're on the witness stand.

Joyce Jillson

Be careful not to impart your wisdom to a guest whose background you do not know. You may be instructing a Nobel Laureate in his own field.

David Brown

The hardest job kids face today is learning good manners without seeing any.

Fred Astaire

Evil

Spock . . . I've found that evil usually triumphs—unless good is very, very careful.

Dr. Leonard McCoy, "Star Trek"

There are no holidays in the fight against evil.

Maxwell Smart, "Get Smart"

All the laws in the world won't stop one man with a gun.

Det. Lt. Mike Stone,
"The Streets of San Francisco"

Evolution

What the caterpillar calls a tragedy, the Master calls a butterfly.

Richard Bach

At one point, Howard, we were hunters and gatherers and then seems like all of a sudden we became party goers.

Jane Wagner

The trouble with the 1980's as compared with the 1970's is that teenagers no longer rebel and leave home.

Marion Smith

Man can only doodle on his napkin for so long.
Remington Steele, "Remington Steele"

Out of every disaster, a little progress is made.
The Control Voice,
"The Outer Limits"

If a plant's roots are too tight. Repot.

The New York Times, Gardening Headline

I think if I got a bicycle from my father, I should give a car to my son.

Lech Walesa

Every problem was once a solution to a previous problem.

Bob Mandel

If evolution was worth its salt, by now it should've evolved something better than survival of the fittest. Yeah, I told 'em I think a better idea would be survival of the wittiest.

Jane Wagner

Excellence

Integrate what you believe into every single area of your life. Take your heart to work and ask the most and best of everybody else. Don't let your special character and values, the secret that you know and no one else does, the truth—don't let that get swallowed up by the great chewing complacency.

Meryl Streep

Learn by practice. Whether it means to learn to dance by practicing dancing or to live by practicing living, the principles are the same. In each, it is the performance of the dedicated precise set of acts, physical or intellectual, from which comes shape of achievement, a sense of one *being*, a satisfaction. One becomes, in some area, an athlete of God.

Martha Graham

If you're lucky enough to find a guy with a lot of head and a lot of heart, he'll never come off the field second.

Vince Lombardi

If your project doesn't work, look for the part that you didn't think was important.

Arthur Bloch

Striving for excellence motivates you; striving for perfection is demoralizing.

Dr. Harriet Braiker

A first rate soup is better than a second rate painting.

Abraham Maslow

We must overcome the notion that we must be regular. It robs us of the chance to be extraordinary and leads us to the mediocre.

Uta Hagen

Let me win, but if I cannot win, let me be brave in the attempt.

Motto, The Special Olympics

Excuses

I am not a crook.

> Richard M. Nixon

How in the hell would I know why there are Nazis? I don't know how this can opener works.

> Leo Postrel to Woody Allen
> *Hannah and Her Sisters*

I hate the beach, I hate the sun. I'm pale and I'm a redhead. I don't tan — I stroke.

> Woody Allen, *Play It Again Sam*

I'm not that bad; I'm just drawn that way.

> Jessica Rabbit (Kathleen Turner)
> *Who Framed Roger Rabbit*

The devil made me do it!

> Flip Wilson as "Ernestine"

Exit Lines

Goodnight Mrs. Calabash, wherever you are.

> Jimmy Durante

Can we have a little traveling music?

> Jackie Gleason

And away we go!

> Jackie Gleason

Let's be careful out there.

> Sgt. Esterhaus, "Hill Street Blues"

Thanks for the memory.

> Song lyric, sung by Bob Hope

Happy trails to you.

> Roy Rogers and Dale Evans

Experience

Experience is not what happens to a man, it's what a man does with what happens to him.

Aldous Huxley

Idealism is what precedes experience; cynicism is what follows.

David T. Wolf

I hate when my foot falls asleep during the day because I know its going to be up all night.

Stephen Wright

Some luck lies in not getting what you thought you wanted but getting what you have, which, once you have got it, you may be smart enough to see is what you would have wanted had you known.

Garrison Keillor

Everything that I loved was taken away from me and I did not die.

Rod Steiger, *The Pawnbroker*

It's all right letting yourself go, as long as you can get yourself back.

Mick Jagger

I cried for the man who had no hair until I met the man with no head.

Bud Lutz, "Eisenhower and Lutz"

There are three things you don't get over in a hurry—losing a woman, eating bad possum, and eating good possum.

Beau LaBarre, "Welcome Back,
Kotter"

A thick skin is a gift from God.

Conrad Adenauer

Trying to define yourself is like trying to bite your own teeth.

Alan Watts

Nobody's heartburn is like your heartburn.

Ad for Gaviscon Antiacid

I've learned that if you want people to join in any kind of conservation effort, you have to help them to care with their hearts, not just their heads.

Jane Goodall

I don't have to have faith, I have experience.

Joseph Campbell

If you know what you're doing, you can be daring.

Gerald Perry Finnerman,
Cinematographer

I quit being afraid when my first venture failed and the sky didn't fall down.

Allen H. Neuharth

Experience, which destroys innocence, also leads one back to it.

James Baldwin

Faith

Eternity is a terrible thought. I mean where's it going to end.

Tom Stoppard

The trouble with born-again Christians is that they are an even bigger pain the second time around.

Herb Caen

Some things have to be believed to be seen.

Ralph Hodgson

Never face facts; if you do you'll never get up in the morning.

Marlo Thomas

Having a dream isn't stupid, Norm. It's not having a dream that's stupid.

Cliff Clavin, "Cheers"

We are called not to be successful but to be faithful.

Ellwood Kieser, C.S.P.

Every human being is born without faith. Faith comes only through the process of making decisions to change before we can be sure it's the right move.

Dr. Robert Schuller

Family

Having a family is like having a bowling alley installed in your brain.

> Martin Mull

When I can no longer bear to think of the victims of broken homes, I begin to think of the victims of intact ones.

> Peter De Vries

Happiness is having a large, loving, caring, close-knit family in another city.

> George Burns

Cleaning your house while your children are still growing is like shoveling the walk before it stops snowing.

> Phyllis Diller

A man can't get rich if he takes proper care of his family.

> Navajo saying

Parents are like cars. . . . built-in obsolescence.
Harvey Lacey, "Cagney & Lacy"

Don't allow no weirdos on the phone unless it's family.
Mama Harper, "Mama's Family"

Let your children go if you want to keep them.
Malcolm Forbes

When you're pants go in the hamper, whatever's inside
becomes public domain.
Valerie Hogan, "Valerie"

Whatever you do to your child's body, you are doing to
your child's mind too.
Penelope Leach

Parenthood remains the greatest single preserve of the
amateur.
Alvin Toffler

Farewells

Everybody has got to die but I've always believed an exception would be made in my case. Now what?

William Saroyan

I'll be right back.

Johnny Carson

Go, and never darken my towels again.

Groucho Marx

In the end, everything is a gag.

Charles Chaplin

A memorial service is a farewell party for somebody who has already left.

Robert Byrne

I'd only blow it.

Robert Redford's last line
to Paul Newman regarding his
share of the take. *The Sting*

Until we meet again, may the good Lord take a liking to you.

Roy Rogers

Fashion

When a popular phenomenon reaches the cover of *Time,* it is already out of fashion.

> R. Holloway

I base my fashion taste on what doesn't itch.

> Gilda Radner

It is better to have poor taste, than no taste at all.

> Unknown

Learn that clothes are there to suit your life, not to run it.

> John Weitz

The well dressed man never stands out in a crowd; his elegance sets him apart.

> Oscar de la Renta

If a woman wants more excitement in her life, she can wear it.

> Margaretha Ley

Women don't wear beautiful lingerie just for men. But thank you anyway.

Christopher Reeves, Ad for Maidenform

Fathers

The most important thing a father can do for his children is love their mother.

Theodore Hesburgh

Don't make a baby if you can't be a Father.

National Urban League Slogan

I grew up to have my father's looks, my father's speech patterns, my father's posture, my father's walk, my father's opinions and my mother's contempt for my father.

Jules Feiffer

Babies don't need fathers, but mothers do. Someone who is taking care of a baby needs to be taken care of.

Amy Heckerling

Fear

We have nothing to fear but sanity itself.

Mork, "Mork & Mindy"

I don't like being afraid. It scares me.

Margaret "Hot Lips"
Houlihan, "M*A*S*H"

The thing we run from is the thing we run to.

Dr. Robert Anthony

Fear is created not by the world around us, but in the mind, by what we think is going to happen.

Elizabeth Gawain

Fear is a question. What are you afraid of and why? Our fears are a treasure house of self knowledge if we explore them.

Marilyn Ferguson

Feelings of inferiority and superiority are the same. They both come from fear.

Dr. Robert Anthony

Fear is faith that it won't work out.

Sister Mary Tricky

We fear the thing we want the most.

Dr. Robert Anthony

Feelings

Pathos is easy to contrive, but it's the pornography of feelings.

> John Young

I feel so bad since you've gone. It's almost like having you here.

> '70s Anonymous

Men who never get carried away should be.

> Malcolm Forbes

It would be a terrible thing to go through life unhappy and not know how miserable you are.

> Frank the gardener,
> "Father Knows Best"

I love getting mail—just the fact that someone licked a stamp for you is very reassuring.

> Thomas Magnum, "Magnum P.I."

My loathings are simple: stupidity, oppression, crime, cruelty, soft music.

> Vladimir Horowitz

Intimacy means "into me see"!

Bob Mandel

One of the quickest ways to feel tired is to suppress your
 feelings.

Sue Patton Thoek

You don't die of a broken heart, you only wish you did.

Marilyn Peterson

Depression occurs when you are not being yourself.

Dennis Wholey

Feminist

Women who seek to be equal with men lack ambition.

Timothy Leary

A feminist man is like a jumbo shrimp, neither makes any sense.

Cassandra Davis,
Comedian

Feminism is doomed to failure because it is based on an attempt to repeal and restructure human nature.

Phyllis Schafley

We're still not where we're going but we're still not where we were.

Natasha Jasefowitz

Remember Ginger Rogers did everything Fred Astaire did, but she did it backwards and in high heels.

Faith Whittlesey

I never realized until lately that women were supposed to be the inferior sex.

Katharine Hepburn

I have met brave women who are exploring the outer edge of human possibility, with no history to guide them and with a courage to make themselves vulnerable that I find moving beyond words.

Gloria Steinem

Film

A movie in production is the greatest train set a boy could ever have.

Orson Welles

At 600 frames per second, you don't screw around with reality.

Lee Philips

A dolly move is a moral commitment.

Bernardo Bertolucci

What you try to become is a bringer of magic, for magic and the truth are closely allied and movies are sheer magic . . . when they work, it's, well, it's glorious.

John Huston

Movies are moments.

Nancy Bein

If you're going to tell people the truth, make them laugh, or they'll kill you.

Billy Wilder

First Amendment

Don't join the bookburners . . . the right to say ideas, the right to record them, and the right to have them accessible to others is unquestioned — or this isn't America.

Dwight D. Eisenhower

Free speech is a right not an obligation.

Graffiti by Leary

Food

We were taken to a fast-food cafe where the order was fed into a computer. Our hamburgers, made from the flesh of chemically impregnated cattle, had been broiled over counterfeit charcoal, placed between slices of artificially flavored cardboard and served to us by recycled juvenile delinquents.

Jean-Michel Chapereau

No one ever filed for divorce on a full stomach.

Mama Leone

I don't even butter my bread. I consider that cooking.

Katherine Cebrian

A gourmet who thinks of calories is like a tart who looks at her watch.

James Beard

It's so beautifully arranged on the plate—you know someone's fingers have been all over it.

Julia Child

We are what we eat.

Adele Davis

When men reach their sixties and retire, they go to pieces. Women go right on cooking.

Gail Sheehy

In Mexico we have a word for sushi: bait.

Jose Simon

If I could have one food for the rest of my life? That's easy. Pez. Cherry-flavored Pez. There's no question about it.

From " *Stand By Me*

Never eat Chinese food in Oklahoma.

Bryan Miller

Six years and you haven't learned anything—it's white wine with Hershey bars!

Harvey Barros, "Making the Grade"

Freedom

The basic test of freedom is perhaps less in what we are free to do than in what we are free not to do.

Eric Hoffer

. . . everything can be taken from a man but one thing: the last of human freedoms — to choose one's attitude in any given set of circumstances — to choose one's own way.

Viktor Frankel

Freedom's just another word for "nothing left to lose."

Song lyric, "Me and Bobby McGee,"
sung by Janis Joplin

You'll never know how sweet freedom can be unless you've lost it for eight and a half years.

Everett Alvarez, Vietnam POW

112

The French

Every Frenchman wants to enjoy one or more privileges;
that way he shows his passion for equality.

Charles de Gaulle

France is the only country where the money falls apart
and you can't tear the toilet paper.

Billy Wilder

A relatively small and eternally quarrelsome country in
Western Europe, fountainhead of rationalist political
manias, militarily impotent, historically inglorious during the past century, democratically bankrupt,
Communist-infiltrated from top to bottom.

William F. Buckley

They aren't much at fighting wars anymore. Despite
their reputation for fashion, their women have spindly
legs. Their music is sappy. But they do know how to
whip up a plate of grub.

Mike Royko

113

Boy those French, they have a different word for everything.

Steve Martin

Friendship

Sometimes you have to get to know someone really well to realize you're really strangers.

Mary Richards, "The Mary
Tyler Moore Show"

Santa Claus has the right idea: visit people once a year.

Victor Borge

A friend is a present you give yourself.

Anonymous

Everybody forgets the basic thing: people are not going to love you unless you love them.

Pat Carroll

Genius

The difference between genius and stupidity is that genius has its limits.

Unknown

Some people possess talent, others are possessed by it. When that happens, a talent becomes a curse.

Rod Serling

God

We have made God into the biggest celebrity of all to contain our own emptiness.

Daniel Boorstin

Christ died for our sins. Dare we make his martyrdom meaningless by not committing them?

Jules Feiffer

God, that dumping ground of our dreams.

Jean Rostand

I am an atheist, thanks be to God.

Luis Bunuel

Jesus: an anarchist who prevailed.

Myers Yori

Everyone in the world is Christ, and they are all crucified.

Sherwood Anderson

God always has another custard pie up His sleeve.
> Lynn Redgrave, *Georgy Girl*

Sometimes I wonder whose side God's on.
> John Wayne, *The Longest Day*

God is just another name for . . . God.
> Cmdr. John Koenig,
> "Space: 1999"

I look at the universe and I know there's an architect.
> Jack Anderson

God don't make no mistakes—that's how he got to be God.
> Archie Bunker, "All in the Family"

My Lord, my Lord! What hath Thou done lately?
> Woody Allen

God is love, but get it in writing.
> Gypsy Rose Lee

I do not believe in God. I believe in cashmere.
> Fran Liebowitz

God knows (She knows) that women try.
> Gloria Steinem

The world is proof that God is a committee.
> Bob Stokes

God doesn't make orange juice; God makes oranges.

Jesse Jackson

If there's no God, then who made Lily Tomlin?

Sister Mary Tricky

Government

The best way to protect the Constitution is to understand it.

> Foundation for the U.S. Constitution

Rudyard Kipling recommended that the leaders of nations study the art of "judicious leaving alone." Chief Justice Berger has a warning sign on his desk: L.I.S. — Let it simmer.

> James Reston

I believe our country is strong enough to be criticized.

> Jack Anderson

Grief

There is a great deal of pain in life and perhaps the only pain that can be avoided is the pain that comes from trying to avoid pain.

R. D. Laing

Grief is a process. If it is allowed, healing will take place naturally.

Hospice of the Foothills

Only the mourning for what one has missed at the crucial time can lead to real healing.

Alice Miller, *Drama of the Gifted Child*

To live is to suffer, to survive is to find meaning in suffering.

Viktor Frankel,
Man's Search for Meaning

Happiness

Happiness is not something you experience, it's something you remember.

Oscar Levant

The only really happy folk are married women and single men.

Unknown

It isn't necessary to be rich and famous to be happy. It's only necessary to be rich.

Alan Alda

If you really want to be happy, nobody can stop you.

Sister Mary Tricky

Happiness is good health and a bad memory.

Ingrid Bergman

Happy people plan actions, they don't plan results.

Dennis Wholey

There is no way to happiness; happiness is the way.

> Dr. Wayne Dyer

All happiness depends on a leisurely breakfast.

> John W. Gardner

To fall in love with yourself is the first secret of happiness. Then if you're not a good mixer you can always fall back on your own company.

> Robert Morley

It is not easy to find happiness in ourselves, and it is impossible to find it elsewhere.

> Agnes Repplier

Happiness is experienced when your life gives you what you are willing to accept.

> Ken Keyes

Happiness is mostly a by-product of doing what makes us feel fulfilled.

> Dr. Benjamin Spock

Caring about others, running the risk of feeling, and leaving an impact on people bring happiness.

> Rabbi Harold Kushner

One of the things I keep learning is that the secret of being happy is doing things for other people.

> Dick Gregory

There are a great many people in our society who are happy, but since they don't know they're happy, they're not happy.

Theodore Isaac Rubin, M.D.

Health

Quit worrying about your health. It'll go away.

Robert Orben

It's no longer a question of staying healthy. It's a question of finding a sickness you like.

Jackie Mason

Smoking is one of the leading causes of statistics.

Fletcher Knebel

I don't jog. If I die, I want to be sick.

Abe Lemons

If you look like your passport photo, you're too ill to travel.

Will Kommen

Allow the disease to heal your life. Begin your journey and become your authentic self. Now.

Bernie Siegal, M.D.

Pathos activates the eyes and ears to see and hear. At times of pathos, illness opens doors to a reality which is closed to a healthy point of view.

Jean Houston

On the quality of life: #1. Realize that each human being has a built-in capacity for recuperation and repair. #2. Recognize that the quality of life is all-important. #3. Assume responsibility for the quality of your own life. #4. Nurture the regenerative and restorative forces within you. #5. Utilize laughter to create a mood in which the other positive emotions can be put to work for yourself and those around you. #6. Develop confidence and ability to feel love, hope and faith, and acquire a strong will to live.

Norman Cousins

We must learn what we fear, that is the case at the core of the restoration of health.

Max Lerner

The only thing harder to get rid of than a winter cold is a 1973 Ford Pinto.

Aileen Foster

Long-range studies imply that doing something with other people, especially something for them, is the most powerful of all stimuli to longevity and health.

Jon Poppy, *Esquire*

I can feel guilty about the past, apprehensive about the future, but only in the present can I act. The ability to be in the present moment is a major component of mental wellness.

Abraham Maslow

Compassion for myself is the most powerful healer of them all.

Theodore Isaac Rubin

One way to get high blood pressure is to go mountain climbing over molehills.

Earl Wilson

Health Food

Like what's the point being a health nut by day if you're a coke head at night.

Jane Wagner

A vegetarian is a person who won't eat anything that can have children.

David Brenner

If bumblebee leavings and stump paste are so good for you, why can't any of those guys (in the health stores) grow full beards?

Calvin Trillin

If I had known I was going to live this long, I'd have taken better care of myself.

Eubie Blake

I don't eat anything that has a face on it.

J. B. Bates

History

There is no humorist like history.

Will and Ariel Durant

History is more or less bunk.

Henry Ford

Whosoever shall not fall by the sword or by famine, shall fall by pestilence, so why bother shaving?

Woody Allen

High insurance rates are what really killed the dinosaurs.

Announcer, "Late Night with David Letterman"

History is the ship carrying living memories into the future.

Stephen Spender

Yeah, I read history. But it doesn't make you nice. Hitler read history, too.

Joan Rivers

Humanity

I worry that humanity has been "advanced" to its present level of incompetency because evolution works on the Peter Principle.

Jane Wagner

There's no map, there's no master plan, there's just people.

Ray, "Stingray"

For a long time now, it appears we've been a species on auto-snooze.

Jane Wagner

Human Nature

Never frighten a little man. He'll kill you.

Robert Heinlein

There are times when you have to choose between being human and having good taste.

Bertolt Brecht

You've always made the mistake of being yourself.

Eugene Ionesco

There are days when it takes all you've got just to keep up with the losers.

Robert Orben

We are what we pretend to be.

Kurt Vonnegut, Jr.

It's relaxing to go out with my ex-wife because she already knows I'm an idiot.

Thomas Warren

Never appeal to a man's better nature. He may not have one. Invoking his self interest gives you more leverage.

Robert Heinlein

People concern themselves with being normal, rather than natural.

Dr. Robert Anthony

I personally think we developed language because of our deep inner need to complain.

Jane Wagner

What's too painful to remember, we just choose to forget.

Song lyric, "The Way We Were,"
Marilyn and Alan Bergman

Strange isn't it, how people manage to ignore those things that they can't understand.

McGee, "Incredible Hulk"

There is a passion in the human heart called aspiration. It flares with a noble flame, and by its light Man has traveled from the caves of darkness to outer space. But when this passion called aspiration becomes lust, when its flame is fanned by greed and private hunger, then aspiration becomes ambition—by which sin the angels fell.

Narrator, "The Outer Limits"

Humility

Humility is no substitute for a good personality.

Jon Winokur

Embarrassment is a good lesson in humility.

Mary's Almanac

Don't be so humble, you're not that great.

Golda Meir

Stay humble. Always answer the phone—no matter who
else is in the car.

Jack Lemmon

Humor

The absolute truth is the thing that makes people laugh.

Carl Reiner

Satire is moral outrage transformed into comic art.

Philip Roth

He who laughs, lasts.

Dr. Robert Anthony

Humorists always sit at the children's table.

Woody Allen

One doesn't have a sense of humor. It has you.

Larry Gelbart

You can teach taste, editorial sense, but the ability to say something funny is something I've never been able to teach anyone.

Abe Burrows

Improvisation is just writing in front of an audience.

Carl Reiner

Humor is the shortest distance between two people.

Victor Borge

Humor is an affirmation of dignity, a declaration to man's superiority to all that befalls him.

Romain Gary

Ideas

When they come, I write them, when they don't come, I don't.

William Faulkner

The human mind treats a new idea the way the body treats a strange protein; it rejects it.

P.B. Medawar, Biologist

Reservations are the condoms in the birth of new ideas.

Twiggy Rathbone, *Hot Metal*

Immortality

I don't want to achieve immortality through my work, I want to achieve immortality by not dying.

Woody Allen

Millions long for immortality who don't know what to do on a rainy Sunday afternoon.

Susan Ertz

A life isn't significant except for its impact on other lives.

Jackie Robinson

Information

A stranger is someone with whom you feel strange.

Bob Mandel

The information we need is not available.
The information we want is not what we need.
The information we have is not what we want.

John Peer

Information is where you find it.

Librarian's Motto

Sometimes a person has to go a very long distance out
of his way to come back a short distance correctly.

Edward Albee

Nothing ever goes away.

Barry Commoner

You don't get to choose how you're going to die. Or
when. You can decide how you're going to live now.

Joan Baez

Poinsettias are the Bob Goulet of botany.

From the play TRU,
by Jay Presson Allen

I don't believe you have to be a cow to know what milk is.

Ann Landers, Time Magazine

Say it loud, say it clear, you can listen as well as you can hear.

Song lyric, "The Living Years,"
Mike & the Mechanics

Flattery is the floating cockroach in the milk of human kindness.

Song lyric, "Hot Metal," Twiggy Rathbone

Always put off until tomorrow what you shouldn't do at all.

Anonymous

If you're more than three feet away from a housefly, it can't see you.

L.M. Boyd

The best way to apply fragrance . . . is to spray it into the air and walk into it.

Estee Lauder

If you paint the inside of your chicken coop orange, you're chickens will lay more eggs.

Anonymous

You'll get more money at resale time if you buy a red car.

P. Lampe

If you slap a cop, you go to jail.

Municipal Judge Rubin
(to Zsa Zsa Gabor)

You don't have to try, you just have to be.

David Viscott

Dreck is dreck and no amount of fancy polish is going to make it anything else.

Linda Ellerbee

In an average life, people spend 101,369,863 hours waiting in line.

Tom Heymann

The more we know, the more we want to know: when we know enough, we know how much we don't know.

Carol Orlock

The future comes one day at a time.

Dean Acheson

Quitting smoking can greatly reduce serious risks to your health.

Warning found on cigarette package

Inspiration

We're on a mission from God.

The Blues Brothers

What do you do when inspiration doesn't come: be careful not to spook, get the wind up, or force things into position. You must wait around until the idea comes.

John Huston

Just don't give up trying to do what you really want to do. Where there is love and inspiration, I don't think you can go wrong.

Ella Fitzgerald

As long as you're going to think anyway, think big.

Donald Trump

You never really lose until you quit trying.

Mike Ditka

If I can make it, you can make it.

Rev. Jesse Jackson

Intelligence

It takes a smart man to know he's stupid.
> Barney Rubble, "The Flintstones"

An intellectual is someone who can listen to the *William Tell* overture and not think of the Lone Ranger.
> Anonymous

I like a woman with a head on her shoulders. I hate necks.
> Steve Martin

International Relations

Men and nations behave wisely once they have exhausted all the other alternatives.

Abba Eban

You can't shake hands with a clenched fist.

Indira Gandhi

The genius of you Americans is that you never make clear-cut stupid moves, only complicated stupid moves which make us wonder at the possibility that there may be something to them which we are missing.

Gamal Nasser

There can be no vulnerability without risk; there can be no community without vulnerability; there can be no peace, and ultimately no life, without community.

M. Scott Peck

There's no difference between one's killing and making decisions that will send others to kill. It's exactly the same thing, or even worse.

Golda Meir

What might save us, me and you, is if the Russians love their children too.

Sting, Song Lyric

We must not be innocents abroad in a world that is not innocent.

Ronald Reagan

You must be very subtle. . . . You have to treat a highly intelligent man as a highly intelligent man. You must make him immediately aware that you are taking him very seriously. And you must enhance his confidence. Flattery is simply to make a man believe he can solve his problems.

Henry Kissinger

Peace between countries must rest on the solid foundation of love between individuals.

Gandhi

Wars don't last forever. Ony war does.
Hawkeye Pierce, "M*A*S*H"

Irony

You write a hit play the same way you write a flop.
                                                    William Saroyan

You get your teeth fixed, your mouth doesn't work.
                                                    Anonymous

A $20 haircut hardly ever lasts longer than a $5 haircut.
                                                    Wes Smith

How can I miss you if you never go away?
                                                    Country Song

You cannot control without being controlled.
                                                    Dr. Robert Anthony

Midgets are the last to know its raining.
                                                    Larry Tucker

Send in the clowns. Don't bother they're here.
                            Song lyric, "Send in the Clowns,"
                                                    Stephen Sondheim

The only way to win a power struggle is to give it up.

Bob Mandel

The trouble with the rat race is that even if you win, you're still a rat.

Lily Tomlin

Everything we say about other people is really about ourselves.

Merrit Malloy

People need each other most when they are at their worst.

From *House of Hearts Book*

The lady with the answers does not have the answer to this one.

Ann Landers, on her divorce

The trouble with unemployment is that the minute you wake up in the morning you're on the job.

Slappy White

My father was often angry when I was most like him.

Lillian Hellman

Two wrongs don't make a right, but three rights will make a left.

Painter's Rule of the Road

The two biggest sellers in any bookstore are the cookbooks and the diet books. The cookbooks tell you how to prepare the food and the diet books tell you how not to eat any of it.

Andy Rooney

Our strength is often composed of the weaknesses we're damned if we're going to show.

Mignon McLaughlin

Sometimes one must cut off a finger to save a hand.

Master Po, "Kung Fu"

Every silver lining has a cloud.

Kerr Avon, "Blake's 7"

No good deed ever goes unpunished.

B.J. Hunnicutt, "M*A*S*H"

It's almost as important to know what is not serious as to know what is.

John Kenneth Galbraith

People think the Beatles know what's going on. We don't. We're just doing it.

John Lennon

Being lost is worth the being found.

Neil Diamond, song lyric

Sacred cows make great hamburgers.

Robert Reisner

A man can be called ruthless if he bombs a country to oblivion. A woman can be called ruthless if she puts you on hold.

Gloria Steinem

Jews

There are very few Japanese Jews. As a result, there is no Japanese word for Alan King.

Johnny Carson

My father never lived to see his dream come true of an all Yiddish speaking Canada.

David Steinberg

Jesus was a Jew, yes, but only on his mother's side.

Archie Bunker, "All in the Family"

Johnson, Lyndon B.

I never trust a man until I've got his pecker in my pocket.

Lyndon B. Johnson

Jerry Ford is a nice guy, but he played too much football with his helmet off.

Lyndon B. Johnson

Kennedy, John F.

Ask not what your country can do for you but what you can do for your country.

John F. Kennedy

What's the use of being Irish if the world doesn't break your heart?

John F. Kennedy

Ich bin ein Berliner.

John F. Kennedy, Berlin speech

Those who make peaceful revolution impossible will make violent revolution inevitable.

John F. Kennedy

Liberty without learning is always in peril; learning without liberty is always in vain.

John F. Kennedy

I think this is the most extraordinary collection of talent, of human knowledge, that has ever been gathered together at the White House, with the possible exception of when Thomas Jefferson dined alone.

John F. Kennedy
(at a dinner for Nobel Prize winners, 1962)

151

For a time we felt this country was ours. Now it's theirs again.

Norman Mailer on JFK's assassination

Knowledge

You can only have two things in life, reasons or results. Reasons don't count.

Dr. Robert Anthony

In the end we will conserve only what we love. We will love only what we understand. We will understand only what we are taught.

Senegalese saying

All I ever needed to know I learned in kindergarten. Don't hit people. Clean up your own mess.

Robert Fulghum

What the student calls a tragedy, the master calls a butterfly.

Richard Bach, *Illusions*

Letting people be okay without us is how we get to be okay without them.

Merrit Malloy

There is no way to know before experiencing.

Dr. Robert Anthony

Knowledge is knowing as little as possible.

Charles Bukowski

As we acquire knowledge, things do not become more comprehensible, but more mysterious.

Will Durant

The Law

The big print giveth and the small print taketh away.
                                        Bishop Fulton Sheen

Getting kicked out of the American Bar Association is like getting kicked out of the Book-of-the-Month Club.
                                        Melvin Belli

Whatever their other contributions to our society, lawyers could be an important source of protein.
                                        Guindon cartoon caption

Divorce is a game played by lawyers.
                                        Cary Grant

I'm not an ambulance chaser. I'm usually there before the ambulance.
                                        Melvin Belli

Broke a mirror in my house and I'm supposed to get seven years bad luck but my lawyer thinks he can get me five.
                                        Stephen Wright

Liberals

The liberals can understand everything but people who don't understand them.

Lenny Bruce

Hell hath no fury like a liberal scorned.

Dick Gregory

Forty-two percent of all liberals are queer. The Wallace people took a poll.

Peter Boyle, *Joe*

Liberals want to manage the damage with government programs to take care of those who have fallen between the cracks. Populists want to fix the cracks so that people don't fall in the first place.

Jim Hightower, Texas
Commissioner of Agriculture

Liberals feel unworthy of their possessions. Conservatives feel they deserve everything they've stolen.

Mort Sahl

Life

Life is short; live it up.

> Nikita Khrushchev

Life is like an overlong drama through which we sit being nagged by the vague memories of having read the reviews.

> John Updike

Life is what happens when you are making other plans.

> John Lennon

Everything has been figured out except how to live.

> Jean-Paul Sartre

Life is too short to stuff a mushroom.

> Storm Jameson

There must be more to life than having everything.

> Maurice Sendak

It's hard to play Hamlet when you know the joke.

> Suzanna Cary

These *are* the good old days.

Carly Simon, song lyric

How can they tell?

Dorothy Parker on being told
of Calvin Coolidge's death.

It ain't over till it's over.

Yogi Berra

Life is not the opposite of death, it is the absence of
death.

Merrit Malloy

Life is a journey, not a destination.

Anonymous

God forbid anything should be easy.

Hawkeye, "M*A*S*H"

Birds sing after a storm, why shouldn't we?

Rose Kennedy

You win some, you lose some, and some get rained out,
but you gotta suit up for them all.

J. Askenberg

The way I see it, if you want the rainbow, you gotta
put up with the rain.

Dolly Parton

No matter how big or soft or warm your bed is, you still have to get out of it.

Grace Slick

Life is just a bag of tricks.

"Felix the Cat"

You don't get to choose how you're going to die. Or when. You can only decide how you are going to live. Now.

Joan Baez

What I want to tell you today is not to move into that world where you're alone with yourself and your mantra and your fitness program or whatever it is that you might use to try to control the world by closing it out. I want to tell you just to live in the mess. Throw yourself out into the convulsions of the world. I'm not telling you to make the world better, because I don't believe progress is necessarily part of the package. I'm telling you to live in it. Try and get it. Take chances, make your own work, take pride in it. Seize the moment.

Joan Didion, Commencement Address

We are born princes and the civilizing process makes us frogs.

Eric Berne

It seems like we have to work at innocence and being pure, and at the same time we have to work at being successful so that we have an understanding as to what the rest of the world is up to.

Brother Anthony Fiore

Life is a gamble at terrible odds. If it was a bet you wouldn't take it.

Tom Stoppard

Here is the test to find whether your mission on earth is finished: If you're alive it isn't.

Richard Bach

Living is a form of not being sure, not knowing what's next or how. The moment you know how you begin to die a little.

Agnes DeMille

Showing up is eighty percent of life.

Woody Allen

When we are not sure, we are alive.

Graham Greene

When you're green, you're growing. When you're ripe, you rot.

Ray Kroc

Life is like a B-grade movie. You don't want to leave in the middle of it, but you don't want to see it again.

Ted Turner

It's not easy being green.

Kermit the Frog

The difference between life and the movies is that a script has to make sense, and life doesn't.

Joseph L. Mankiewicz

Logic

If the world were a logical place, men would ride side-saddle.

Rita Mae Brown

If it isn't at the 7-11, I don't need it.

Marilyn Peterson

I never believed in Santa Claus because I knew no white dude would come into my neighborhood after dark.

Dick Gregory

We've got to believe in free will, we have got no choice.

Isaac Bashevis Singer

Asked why he robbed banks, the notorious American bank robber Willie Sutton is reputed to have remarked, "Because that's where the money is."

Theodore White

What is is and what isn't ain't.

Werner Erhard

As for logic, it is in the eye of the logician.

Gloria Steinem

Hypothetical questions get hypothetical answers.

Joan Baez

You can't have everything. Where would you put it?

Stephen Wright

If most auto accidents happen within five miles of home, why don't we move ten miles away?

Michael Davis, "Tonight Show"

In life, everything is one of two things—either everything is exactly as it seems or nothing is as it seems. The trick is to know which.

Susan Profit, "Wiseguy"

That's why they made tomorrow—so we don't have to do everything today.

Betty Jones, "Barnaby Jones"

I know there are blue berries, but they might not be blueberries. And while all blueberries are not blue berries, not all blue berries are blueberries.

Alex Reiger, "Taxi"

Apart from the known and the unknown, what else is there?

Harold Pinter

Once the toothpaste is out of the tube, it's hard to get it
  back in.

H.R. Haldeman

You get to be there first by getting there first.

Federal Express Ad

Loneliness

The eternal quest of the individual human being is to shatter his loneliness.

> Norman Cousins

If you are lonely while you're alone, you are in bad company.

> Jean-Paul Sartre

Loneliness and the feeling of being unwanted is the most terrible poverty.

> Mother Teresa

Language has created the word "loneliness" to express the pain of being alone, and the word "solitude" to express the glory of being alone.

> Paul Tillich

Los Angeles

I mean, who would want to live in a place where the only cultural advantage is that you can turn right on a red light?

Woody Allen

The town is an advertisement for itself; none of its charms are left to the visitor's imagination.

Christopher Isherwood

L.A.: where there's never weather, and walking is a crime. L.A.: where the streetlights and palm trees go on forever, where darkness never comes, like a deal that never goes down, a meeting that's never taken. The City of Angels: where every cockroach has a screenplay and even the winos wear roller skates. It's that kind of town.

Ian Shoales

Perhaps there is no life after death . . . there's just Los Angeles.

Rich Anderson

Fall is my favorite season in Los Angeles, watching the birds change colors and fall from the trees.

David Letterman

There are two million interesting people in New York and only seventy-eight in Los Angeles.

Neil Simon

Nothing is wrong with Southern California that a rise in the ocean level wouldn't cure.

Ross McDonald

Love

Nothing spoils the taste of peanut butter like unre-
quited love.

> Charlie Brown

It's possible to love a human being if you don't know
them too well.

> Charles Bukowski

Money is a powerful aphrodisiac. But flowers work
almost as well.

> Robert Heinlein

Love doesn't care what we call it.

> Gerald Jampolsky

Love is so much better when you're not married.

> Maria Callas

No matter how it looks to us, love never loses control; the laws of our relations are as honest and as exact as the laws of physics.

> Thaddeus Golas

I'm not saying my relationship with Marion Davies is right; I'm saying it is.

> William Randolph Hearst

Love is never having to say you're sorry.

> Erich Segal

All you need is love, love is all you need.

> Song lyric by the Beatles

What's love got to do with it?

> Song lyric, sung by Tina Turner

In expressing love, we belong among the undeveloped countries.

> Saul Bellow

You don't have to go looking for love when it is where you come from.

> Werner Erhard

Love, it is a flower and you its only seed.

> Song lyric, "The Rose,"
> Amanda McBroom

We almost made it but we wanted it all.

> From the song "We Wanted It All,"
> Burt Bachrach & Carole Bayer Sager

Anywhere you go, let me go too. Love me, that's all I ask of you.

> From *Phantom of the Opera,*
> Andrew Lloyd Webber

True love comes quietly, without banners or flashing lights. If you hear bells, get your ears checked.

> Erich Segal

Love is as strict as acting. If you want to love some-body, stand there and do it. If you don't, don't. There are no other choices.

> Tyne Daly

To love is to stop comparing.

> Merrit Malloy

I don't want clever conversation,
I never want to work that hard,
I just want someone I can talk to,
I want you just the way you are.

> Billy Joel, "Just the Way You Are"

Jealousy is not a barometer by which the depth of love can be read. It merely records the degree of the lover's insecurity.

> Margaret Mead

Age doesn't protect you from love. But love, to some extent, protects you from age.

Jeanne Moreau

Love ain't nothin' but sex misspelled.

Harlan Ellison

Hate is not the opposite of love, apathy is.

Rollo May

In the end, the love you get is equal to the love you make.

Song lyric, "Abbey Road," Paul McCartney

For finally, we are as we love. It is love that measures our stature.

William Sloane Coffin

Can't get used to something so right.

Paul Simon, song lyric

Love is nature's psychotherapy.

Eric Berne

It takes a lot of mulch, love does, to create a froth.

Merle Shain

Love is the part of us that is real.

Gerald Jampolsky

Ultimately, love is self approval.

Sondra Ray

I just want you to love me, primal doubts and all.

William Holden as Max Schumacher
in *Network*

Lunatics

To avoid lunatics on city buses, sit in the middle of the bus.

Keith Hunter

When we talk to God, we're praying. When God talks to us, we're schizophrenic.

Jane Wagner

Malapropisms

I'm just trying to simulate some thinking on this sub-ject.

Anonymous

We shouldn't sit back on our hunches and not do any-thing.

Anonymous

These figures might be right cause they pretty much jive.

Anonymous

It's a proven fact that capital punishment is a known detergent against crime.

Archie Bunker, "All in the Family"

What's this I hear about making Puerto Rico a steak? The next thing they'll be wanting is a salad, and then a baked potato.

Gilda Radner as "Emily Litella,"<br>"Saturday Night Live"

The loss of life will be irreplaceable.

> Dan Quayle, regarding San Francisco
> earthquake tragedy

I stand by my misstatements.

> Dan Quayle

Don't forget to miss it.

> Dizzy Dean

The holocaust is the worst thing that ever happened to the people of this country.

> Dan Quayle

A verbal agreement isn't worth the paper it's written on.

> Samuel Goldwyn

Marriage

Marriage is like paying an endless visit in your worst clothes.

> J.B. Priestley

Who wears the pants in this house? I do, and I also wash and iron them.

> Dennis Thatcher,
> husband of Margaret

The surest way to be alone is to get married.

> Gloria Steinem

I've been married most of my life. And when you're married, you don't have sex.

> Zsa Zsa Gabor

If marriage were only bed, we could have made it.

> Marilyn Monroe
> of Joe DiMaggio

Aim high but marry rich.

> Mother Bear

I couldn't see tying myself down with a middle-aged woman with four children, even though the woman was my wife and the children were my own.

Joseph Heller

Many a man owes his success to his first wife and his second to his success.

Jim Backus

I tended to place my wife under a pedestal.

Woody Allen

We want playmates we can own.

Jules Feiffer

A person who has been married many years knows more about marriage than one who has been married many times.

Anonymous

In marriage it is all very well to say that "the two are made one," the question is—which one?

Anonymous

Marriage is not merely sharing the fettucini, but sharing the burden of finding the fettucini restaurant in the first place.

Calvin Trillin

I'm very old-fashioned. I believe that people should stay married for life, like pigeons and Catholics.

Woody Allen

Marriage is like the Middle East—no solutions.

Shirley Valentine

Marriage is really tough because you have to deal with feelings and lawyers.

Richard Pryor

I want to tell you the truth about marriage, son: it's impossible. As impossible as making it into the big leagues. As impossible as making a million dollars. As impossible as doing the right things for your kids so that when they grow up, they love you as much as you love them. And the damn catch is that the only thing that keeps us from being a nation of empty suits is that every now and then we go for the impossible. And today, son, you're going for the impossible.

John Lucey, "Dear John"

I don't want to be married. I don't know—it sounds crazy, but in my mind, it's all connected. You get married, you have kids, you grow old, then you die. Somehow, it seems to me, if you didn't get married, you wouldn't die.

John Burns, "Taxi"

Trust your husband, adore your husband, and get as much as you can in your own name.

Joan Rivers

Why can't somebody invent something for us to marry besides women.

Fred Flintstone, "The Flintstones"

I'd like to get married because I like the idea of a man being required by law to sleep with me every night.

Carrie Snow

How dear of you to let me out of jail.

Katharine Hepburn, *The Lion in Winter*

That shows how long we've been married. Now you kiss me to calm me down.

Joan Davis

Marriage is a big step . . . even for a horse.

Wilbur, "Mr. Ed"

It is threads, hundreds of tiny threads, which sew people together through the years. That's what makes a marriage last more than passion or sex.

Simone Signoret

Why get married and make one man miserable when I can stay single and make thousands miserable.

Carrie Snow

I've been married fifty-five years and I've been home three weeks.

Bob Hope

Marriage may restrict your activity, but it increases your pleasure. It permits sex without shame, fear, or guilt.

Rev. Robert Schuller

You can't bond with a male until you set your parents
free.

Bob Mandel

Maturity

I was always taught to respect my elders and I've now reached the age when I don't have anybody to respect.

George Burns

The true test of maturity is not how old a person is but how he reacts to awakening in the mid-town area in his shorts.

Woody Allen

I still want to play music but I don't want to look like Donald Duck while I'm doing it.

Elton John

Marriage is our last best chance to grow up.

Joseph Barth

Is old age really so terrible? Not if you've brushed your teeth faithfully.

Woody Allen

Smoking is, as far as I'm concerned, the entire point of being an adult.

Fran Liebowitz

Growing up is after all only the understanding that one's unique and incredible experience is what everyone shares.

Doris Lessing

When you make a world tolerable for yourself, you make a world tolerable for others.

Anais Nin

One sign of maturity is knowing when to ask for help.

Dennis Wholey

What we are is our parents' children; what we become is our children's parents.

Merrit Malloy

Medicine

A male gynecologist is like an auto mechanic who has never owned a car.

Carrie Snow

Never argue with a doctor; he has inside information.

Bob & Ray

All them surgeons—they're highway robbers. Why do you think they wear masks when they work on you?

Archie Bunker,
"All in the Family"

Never deny a diagnosis, but do deny the negative verdict that may go with it.

Norman Cousins

For 30 years my patients have walked out on me. And I'm proud of it.

Dr. Allan Elfant, Podiatrist

Men

The bravest thing that men do is love women.

Mort Sahl

A girl can wait for the right man to come along but in the meantime that still doesn't mean she can't have a wonderful time with all the wrong ones.

Cher

Eventually all men come out of the bathroom dressed as a majorette.

Ernestyne White

Men have always been afraid that women could get along without them.

Margaret Mead

I like men to behave like men—strong and childish.

Francoise Sagan

Men are more sentimental than women. It blurs their thinking.

Robert Heinlein

Jewish men don't know anything.

Marilyn Monroe

I met a guy who drives a truck. He can't tell time but he sure can drive.

From the song
"I Like 'Em Big and Stupid,"
sung by Julie Brown

If anything happens to me tell every woman I've ever gone out with I was talking about her at the end. That way they'll have to reevaluate me.

Albert Brooks to Holly Hunter,
Broadcast News

There she was: dejected, desperate, and stoned. Everything I could have hoped for in a woman.

Louis DePalma, "Taxi"

Men are such idiots and I married their king.

Peg Bundy, "Married with
Children"

Men are nothing but lazy lumps of drunken flesh. They crowd you in bed, get you all worked up, and then before you can say "Is that all there is?" that's all there is.

Mrs. Gravas (Latka's mother)
"Taxi"

Can you imagine a world without men? No crime and lots of happy fat women.

Marion Smith

If a man's a good kisser, he's a great f—.

Cher

A good man doesn't just happen. They have to be created by a woman. A guy is a lump like a doughnut. So, first you gotta get rid of all the stuff his mom did to him. And then you gotta get rid of all that macho crap that they pick up from the beer commercials. And then, there's my personal favorite, the male ego.

Roseanne Barr

Just be considerate, accept each other for what you are, and don't point out the fact that the hair he's losing on his head is now growing out of his nose — and his ears.

Peg Bundy, "Married with Children"

Until men can become pregnant, we will not have effective birth control.

Anonymous

To women, we are like big dogs that talk.

Comic Larry Miller

Every man sees a little of himself in Rhett Butler.

Ted Turner

You're not too smart, I like that in a man.

Kathleen Turner, *Body Heat*

I'd know him in the dark.

Ad for Calvin Klein's "Obsession" for men.

Every boy, in his heart, would rather steal second base than an automobile.

Tom Clark

Some men are more perfect than others.

Merle Shain

There are men too gentle to live among wolves.

James Kavanaugh

If it wasn't for women, men would still be hanging from trees.

Marilyn Peterson

Military

If General Haig is so smart, why did he finish 214th (out of 310) in his graduating class at West Point? Does that mean there are 213 generals his age who are smarter than he is?

> Calvin Trillin

Ze soldiers are very hoppy shooting ze pipples who say that ze pipples are not hoppy.

> George Hamilton, *Zorro,*
> *The Gay Blade*

Rommel, you beautiful bastard, I read your book.

> George C. Scott, *Patton*

Anyone who wants to get out of combat isn't really crazy, so I can't ground him.

> Jack Gilford to Alan Arkin,
> *Catch-22*

Miscellaneous

Say what you will about Leona Helmsley, when it comes to standing trial, she's twice the man Jim Bakker is.

David Letterman

Except for socially, you're my role model.

Joan Cusack to Holly Hunter,
Broadcast News

I got tides to regulate! I got no time for flatulence and orgasms.

Robin Williams' detached head
to his errant body in *The
Adventures of Baron Munchausen*

Money

Money is not everything, but it is better than having one's health.

Woody Allen

The richer your friends, the more they will cost you.

Elizabeth Marbury

Never invest your money in anything that eats or needs repairing.

Billy Rose

I have enough money to last me the rest of my life— unless I buy something.

Jackie Mason

Better to be nouveau than never to have been rich at all.

Anonymous

Money is a good thing to have. It frees you from doing things you dislike. Since I dislike doing nearly everything, money is handy.

Groucho Marx

The only way a poor man can make it nowadays is to have a lot of money.

> Blake, "O'Henry"

I started out with nothing. I still have most of it.

> Michael Davis, "Tonight Show"

Money can't buy happiness. . . . But then, happiness can't buy government-insured C.D.'s.

> David Addison, "Moonlighting"

Money speaks all languages.

> J.R. Ewing, "Dallas"

I'm mad that money counts for everything in this world—and that I don't have any.

> Alex Reiger, "Taxi"

Money talks but it can't sing and dance and it don't walk.

> Song lyric, sung by Neil Diamond

Money is good for bribing yourself through the inconveniences of life.

> Gottfried Reinhardt

A reminder to everyone spending money like there's no tomorrow. There is a tomorrow.

> Ad for Chase Manhattan Bank

Since I'm known as a 'rich person', I feel I have to tip at least $5 each time I check my coat. On top of that, I would have to wear a very expensive coat, and it would have to be insured. Added up, without a top-coat I save over $20,000 a year.

Aristotle Onassis

Money can't buy happiness but it will get you a better class of memories.

Ronald Reagan

I know a fellow who's as broke as the Ten Commandments.

John P. Marquand

If you know how people feel about money, that's more revealing than any other single thing I know, including sleeping with them.

Jerry Sterner

Bankruptcy is a legal proceeding in which you put your money in your pants pocket and give your coat to the creditors.

Joey Adams

Morality

Never let your sense of morals interfere with doing the right thing.

John Peer

Immorality: the morality of those who are having a better time.

Unknown

The wicked at heart probably know something.

Woody Allen

A man can have two, maybe three love affairs while he's married. After that, it's cheating.

Yves Montand

If you don't stand for something, you'll fall for anything.

Michael Evans

There's right and there's wrong. You get to do one or the other. You do the one, and you're living. You do the other, and you may be walking around but you're dead as a beaver hat.

John Wayne

To avert disaster, we have not only to teach men to make things but to teach them to have complete moral control over what they make.

Charles, Prince of Wales

Words can hit a child as hard as a fist. Stop using words that hurt.

Ad Council

The one thing that doesn't abide by majority rule is a person's conscience.

Harper Lee

Mothers

I figure if the kids are alive at the end of the day, I've done my job.

Roseanne Barr

It's not easy being a mother. If it were, fathers would do it.

Dorothy, "The Golden Girls"

I know how to do anything—I'm a mom.

Roseanne Barr

Music

God invented rock 'n' roll so kids could hear him.

"Mac" Malloy

Classical music is music written by famous dead foreigners.

Arlene Smith

Listening to the Fifth Symphony of Ralph Vaughn Williams is like staring at a cow for forty-five minutes.

Aaron Copland

Rock and roll is the hamburger that ate the world.

Peter York

MTV is the lava lamp of the 1980's.

Doug Ferrari

Taken together, our songs are like a mural of our lives.

Vernon Reid, "Living Colour"

As far as I'm concerned, there won't be a Beatles reunion as long as John Lennon remains dead.

George Harrison

Nature

I have a seashell collection; maybe you've seen it? I keep it on beaches all over the world.

Stephen Wright

Civilization exists by geological consent, subject to change without notice.

Will Durant

The world is not to be put in order, the world is order. It is for us to put ourselves in unison with this order.

Henry Miller

Nature bats last.

Bumper Sticker

Neo-Cliches

Have a nice day!

                                        Anonymous

Have a day.

                                        Joseph Ingolf

You can trust me.

                                        Joe Izuzu

Shit happens!

                                        '80s motto

Life is hard, then you die.

                                        '80s motto

Go ahead, make my day!

                                        Clint Eastwood,
                                        Sudden Impact

Are we having fun yet?

                                        Carol Burnett,
                                        The Four Seasons

E.T. phone home.

ET

May the force be with you.

Star Wars

My father made him an offer he couldn't refuse.

Al Pacino to Diane Keaton,
The Godfather

The secret of survival is: Always expect the unexpected.

Dr. Who

Where's the beef?

Ad for Wendy's Hamburger

New Age

Enlightenment is any experience of expanding our consciousness beyond its present limits.

Thaddeus Golas

God didn't make junk.

Terry Cole-Whittaker

One night I stayed up all night playing poker with tarot cards. I got a full house and four people died.

Stephen Wright

New York

New York now leads the world's great cities in the number of people around whom you shouldn't make a sudden move.

David Letterman

If you get caught between the moon and New York City, the best that you can do is fall in love.

Song lyric, "Arthur's Theme,"
Arthur

This warning from the New York City Department of Health Fraud: Be suspicious of any doctor who tries to take your temperature with his finger.

David Letterman

If you can make it there, you'll make it anywhere.

Song lyric, "New York, New York"

Someone did a study of the three most-often-heard phrases in New York City. One is "Hey taxi." Two is "What train do I take to get to Bloomingdales?" And three is "Don't worry, it's only a flesh wound."

David Letterman

Don't even think of parking here.

N.Y. Police Dept. sign
at bus stop

Tip to out-of-town visitors. If you buy something here in New York and you want to have it shipped home, be suspicious if the clerk tells you they don't need your name and address.

David Letterman

Every year when it's Chinese New Year here in New York, there are fireworks going off at all hours. New York mothers calm their frightened children by telling them it's just gunfire.

David Letterman

Nixon, Richard M.

When a president does it, then it is not illegal.

Richard M. Nixon

You won't have Richard Nixon to kick around anymore.

Richard M. Nixon

Paranoia

A paranoid is a man who knows a little of what's going on.

William Burroughs

Even paranoids have real enemies.

Delmore Schwartz

I am a kind of paranoid in reverse. I suspect people of plotting to make me happy.

J.D. Salinger

When everyone is out to get you, paranoia is only good thinking.

Johnny Fever, "WKRP Cincinnati"

Peace

If there is any peace it will come through being, not knowing.

Henry Miller

People in the long run are going to do more to promote peace than governments.

Dwight David Eisenhower

What all men are really after is some form, or perhaps only some formula, of peace.

Joseph Conrad

Perseverance

Concentrated effort along a single line of endeavor is boring, but it makes people rich.

Lee Winkler

We came, we saw, we kicked its ass!

Bill Murray, *Ghostbusters*

Don't be afraid to give up the good to go for the great.

Kenny Rogers

You do what you can for as long as you can, and when you finally can't, you do the next best thing. You back up but you don't give up.

Chuck Yeager

As we say in the sewer, if you're not prepared to go all the way, don't put your boots on in the first place.

Ed Norton, "The Honeymooners"

Philosophy

I can, therefore, I am.

Simone Weil

I reek, therefore I am.

Diane Chambers, "Cheers"

I yam what I yam and that's all I yam.

Popeye

I have a new philosophy. I am only going to dread one
day at a time.

Charles Schultz

Remembering is the opposite of being here now; it's
being there now.

Merrit Malloy

The object of philosophy is the logical clarification of
thought.

Ludwig Wittgenstein

It's a small world but I wouldn't want to paint it.

Stephen Wright

I've distilled everything to one simple principle: win or die!

Glenn Close, *Dangerous Liaisons*

I'm not a minority. I'm an outnumbered majority.

"Chico and the Man"

Bite your tongue. Get a cinder in your eye. When you feel good, you feel nothing.

R. Buckminster Fuller

You must be either a hammer or an anvil.

#6, "The Prisoner"

Never give up: and never, under any circumstances, no matter what—never face the facts.

Ruth Gordon

Don't worry. Be happy.

Song lyric, Bobby McFerrin

Poetry

Poetry is rapture. Without it, we are doomed.

From *Dead Poet's Society*

In communist countries, you execute your poets. In the free world, the poets execute themselves.

Kate Braverman

When power leads men towards arrogance, poetry reminds him of his limitations. When power narrows the area of man's concern, poetry reminds him of the richness and diversity of existence. When power corrupts, poetry cleanses.

John F. Kennedy

Police

You know, if you shoot me you'll lose a lot of these humanitarian awards.

Chevy Chase as *Fletch*

Your tragedy is our incentive; we just love to see nice people get into trouble.

Arthur Dietrich, "Barney Miller"

Politicians

My definition of a redundancy is an airbag in a politician's car.

Larry Hagman

Ninety percent of the politicians give the other ten percent a bad reputation.

Henry Kissinger

Never ask poets about politics or politicians about poetry.

Shauna Sorensen

I always wanted to get into politics, but I was never light enough to make the team.

Art Buchwald

Old Prayer for Politicians: Teach us to utter words that are tender and gentle. Tomorrow we may have to eat them.

Morris Udall

Politics

It is dangerous for a national candidate to say things that people might remember.

Eugene McCarthy

Anybody that wants the presidency so much that he'll spend two years organizing and campaigning for it is not to be trusted with the office.

David Broder

In order to become the master, the politician poses as the servant.

Charles De Gaulle

Vote Yes on No.

Ernestyne White

The secret of the demagogue is to make himself as stupid as his audience so that they believe they are as clever as he.

Karl Kraus

In politics if you want anything said, ask a man; if you want anything done, ask a woman.

Margaret Thatcher

Communism is like one big phone company.

Lenny Bruce

Walter Mondale has all the charisma of a speed bump.

Will Durst

History must judge John F. Kennedy not only by what he was able to accomplish in a thousand days, but also by what he inspired all of us to volunteer to do for our country.

Thomas M. Scanlon

Get all the fools on your side and you can be elected to anything.

Frank Dane

The way I read Billy Carter's testimony, he was a model citizen himself until the voters went and ruined his life by making his brother President.

Calvin Trillin

Dukakis is the Greek word for Mondale.

Jay Leno

What you always do before you make a decision is consult. The best public policy is made when you are listening to people who are going to be impacted. Then, once a policy is determined, you call on them to help you sell it.

Elizabeth H. Dole

We've got to go to the people with bold ideas and candidates of conviction—we've got to be hotter than high school love.

Jim Hightower, Texas
Commissioner of Agriculture

A cardinal rule of politics—never get caught in bed with a live man or a dead woman.

J.R. Ewing, "Dallas"

When I was in the third grade, there was a kid running for office. His slogan was: "Vote for me and I'll show you my wee-wee." He won by a landslide.

Dorothy Zbornack, "The Golden Girls"

Don't run a campaign that would embarrass your mother.

Senator Robert C. Byrd

In politics one must deal with skunks, but no one should be fool enough to allow the skunks to choose the weapons.

Joe Cannon

There's nothing in the middle of the road but yellow stripes and dead armadillos.

Jim Hightower, Texas
Commissioner of Agriculture

If children could vote, Jesse Jackson would be our next
president.

Frederick Allen

The job of a citizen is to keep his mouth open.

Gunter Grass

Power

Now when I bore people at a party they think it's their fault.

> Henry Kissinger

Power is the ability not to have to please.

> Elizabeth Janeway

Decide exactly what you want to achieve. Do you want to help people, or do you want to be powerful?

> Mario Cuomo

The men who create power make an indispensable contribution to the nation's greatness. But the men who question power make a contribution just as indispensable for they determine whether we use power or power uses us.

> John F. Kennedy

Prejudice

I am not an animal!

John Hurt, *Elephant Man*

Have you always been a Negro, or are you just trying to be fashionable?

Dr. Morton Chesley, "Julia"

Bigotry started a long time ago—nobody knows where. Personally, I think the French started it.

Johnny Fever, "WKRP Cincinnati"

I got nothin' against mankind. It's people I can't stand.

Archie Bunker, "All in the Family"

It's only common sense. If God wanted people to be gay, He wouldn't have created Adam and Eve. He would have created Adam and Steve.

Arthur Harmon, "Maude"

Presidents

As far as the men who are running for President are concerned, they aren't even people I would date.

Nora Ephron

In 1932, lame duck president Herbert Hoover was so desperate to remain in the White House that he dressed up as Eleanor Roosevelt. When FDR discovered the hoax in 1936, the two men decided to stay together for the sake of the children.

Johnny Carson

Nixon, Ford, Carter, Reagan—a Mount Rushmore of incompetence.

David Steinberg

If President Lincoln were alive today, he'd roll over in his grave.

Gerald R. Ford

How far would Moses have gone if he had taken a poll in Egypt?

Harry S. Truman

Read my lips. No new taxes.

President George Bush

The Press

Taking pleasure in the dark side may be some sort of occupational hazard for reporters.

Calvin Trillin

Real news is bad news.

Marshall McLuhan

Before I go out to take a picture of someone, I just stop at the city desk and say, "Do you want him gazing out toward the sunset or picking his nose?"

Photojournalist overhead by
Calvin Trillin

The medium is the message.

Marshall McLuhan

There is nothing personal about a personal ad.

Wes Smith

In dealing with the press, do yourself a favor, stick with one of three responses: (a) I know and I can tell you; (b) I know and I can't tell you; (c) I don't know.

Dan Rather

If you've got some news that you don't want to get noticed, put it out Friday afternoon 4:00 pm.

David Gergen

When you're talking to the media, be a well, not a fountain.

Michael Deaver

You can write a column about one thing, or you can write a column about three things, and tie them up with an over-arching theme. But a two-thing column will never hang together.

Suzanne Garment

Get it first, but first get it right.

Seymour Berkson, INS

When a boy tells a lie, it can cause trouble, but when a newspaper tells a lie, it can cause more trouble. People are liable to find the newspaper a hundred years from now and believe it.

"Wyatt Earp"

Rules for a White House Spokesman: No. 1 is always tell the truth. I've got only one currency, that's the truth. There are 10,000 ways to say "no comment," and I've used 9,999 of them. The second rule is don't be afraid to say, "I don't know." You may look dumb, but if you don't know you can't give them hot air because it always shows on your face.

Larry Speakes

Never argue with people who buy ink by the gallon.

Tommy Lasorda

Problems

If olive oil comes from olives, then where does baby oil come from?

Jane Wagner

The big cities of America are becoming Third World countries.

Nora Ephron

When I'm working on a problem, I never think about beauty. I think only of how to solve the problem; but when I have finished, if the solution is not beautiful, I know it is wrong.

Richard Buckminster Fuller

The Rule of Accuracy: When working toward the solution of a problem, it always helps if you know the answer.

John Peer

If you find a good solution and become attached to it, the solution may become your next problem.

Dr. Robert Anthony

If you get to be a really big headliner, you have to be prepared for people throwing bottles at you in the night.

Mick Jagger

She was in perfect condition except for one thing—she was dead.

"Quincy"

When you're ready to do something about a problem, almost anything can help. When you're not ready, no amount of workshops, counselling or programs will effect a change. The rule is: "When a student is ready, the teacher appears."

Andrew Franken

Prophesy

Build it and he will come...

The Voice, Field of Dreams

You may say I'm a dreamer but I'm not the only one. I hope someday you'll join us and the world will live as one.

Song lyric, "Imagine,"
John Lennon

I've seen the future! It's a bald-headed man from New York!

Albert Brooks, Lost in America

Just remember, in the winter, far beneath the winter's snow
Lies the seed that with the sun's love, in the spring, becomes the rose.

Song lyric, "The Rose,"
Amanda McBroom

It isn't necessary to come true if we are true.

Mary's Almanac

Providence

Once you accept an idea it's an idea whose time has come.

Dr. Robert Anthony

Lead me not into temptation; I can find the way myself.

Rita Mae Brown

Nobody has to tell you when it's right.

'80s Anonymous

Psychology

Life hardly ever lives up to our anxieties.

Paul Monash

Freud is the father of psychoanalysis. It has no mother.

Germaine Greer

Psychoanalysis makes quite simple people feel they're complex.

S.N. Behrman

I'm going to my psychoanalyst one more year, then I'm going to Lourdes.

Woody Allen

Who we are never changes. Who we think we are does.

Mary's Almanac

A kleptomaniac is a person who helps himself because he can't help himself.

Henry Morgan

The best way to deal with somebody is to deal with yourself.

Terry Cole-Whittaker

After a year in therapy, my psychiatrist said to me, "Maybe life isn't for everyone."

Larry Brown

We have met the enemy and he is us.

Pogo

Roses are red, violets are blue, I'm schizophrenic, and so am I.

Frank Crow

Nostalgia is just another form of depression.

Al Giordino, *People* Magazine

Listening, not imitation, may be the sincerest form of flattery.

Dr. Joyce Brothers

Beware of the danger signals that flag problems: silence, secretiveness, or sudden outburst.

Sylvia Porter

When you can't remember why you're hurt, that's when you're healed. When you have to work real hard to re-create the pain, and you can't quite get there, that's when you're better.

Jane Fonda

Neurotic means he is not as sensible as I am, and psychotic means that he is even worse than my brother-in-law.

Karl Menninger

Insanity; a perfectly rational adjustment to the insane world.

R.D. Laing

Guilt is the mafia of the mind.

Bob Mandel

Publicity

Will somebody tell me what kind of a world we live in where somebody dressed up like a bat gets all my press?

The Joker, *Batman*

A boy has to peddle his book.

Truman Capote

Questions

You can't have everything. Where would you put it?
                                        Stephen Wright

Why do they call it the rush hour when nothing moves?
                                        Mork, "Mork & Mindy"

If Hugh Hefner truly thinks that being publicly spread-eagled is so fantasic, how come we haven't seen his little wahoo with a staple in the middle?
                                        Julia Sugarbaker, "Designing Women"

Could Faulkner find a publisher now?
                                        Annie Dillard

Ebony and Ivory
 Live together in perfect harmony
 Side by side on my piano keyboard
 Oh Lord, why don't we?
                                        Song lyric, "Ebony and Ivory"
                                        Paul McCartney

If dreaming is all your subconscious desires coming out, why do people wait 'til they're asleep to do it?

> Max Headroom, "The Max Headroom Show"

If closeness is wrong, why are we born with arms? Isn't that sort of Zen-like?

> Mork, "Mork & Mindy"

Why is it that in 7-Eleven stores, they've got $10,000 worth of cameras watching twenty cents' worth of Twinkies?

> Jay Leno

If you shoot a mime, should you use a silencer?

> Stephen Wright

What is "martinizing" and why does it only take one hour?

> Bill Maher, comic

Reagan, Ronald

Ronald Reagan is not a typical politician because he doesn't know how to lie, cheat, and steal. He always had an agent for that.

Bob Hope

Sure Reagan promised to take senility tests. But what if he forgets?

Lorna Kerr-Walker

Nancy Reagan fell down and broke her hair.

Johnny Carson

Ronald Reagan is a triumph of the embalmer's art.

Gore Vidal

Ronald Reagan has held the two most demeaning jobs in the country—President of the United States and radio broadcaster of the Chicago Cubs.

George Will

I have learned that one of the most important rules of politics is poise — which means looking like an owl after you've behaved like a jackass.

Ronald Reagan

A president should never say never.

Ronald Reagan

Mr. Gorbachev, tear down this wall.

Ronald Reagan,
on Berlin Wall

Reality

After all, what is reality anyway? Nothin' but a collective hunch.

Jane Wagner

All God's children are not beautiful. Most of God's children are, in fact, barely presentable.

Fran Liebowitz

If you have a job without aggravation, you don't have a job.

Malcolm Forbes

Things are not what they seem, they are what they are.

Dr. Robert Anthony

Reality is for people who can't handle drugs.

'70s Anonymous

Unless you have talent, all the experience in the world doesn't mean a thing.

Phil Lathrop
Ad for Eastman Kodak

No matter where you go or what you do, you're gonna die.

Olympia Dukakis, *Moonstruck*

Ya can't learn to be real. It's like learning to be a midget. It's not something you can learn.

Purple Rose of Cairo

Insurance is no substitute for a good alarm system and a twelve gauge shotgun.

Vincent Isbecki, "Cagney & Lacey"

Behind every dark cloud, there's usually rain.

Mike Nesmith, "The Monkees"

Cloquet hated reality but realized it was still the only place to get a good steak.

Woody Allen

What we call reality is an agreement that people have arrived at to make life more livable.

Louise Nevelson

Facts do not cease to exist because they are ignored.

Aldous Huxley

Regrets

My one regret in life is that I am not someone else.

Woody Allen

Nostalgia isn't what it used to be.

Simone Signoret

When I first came into this world, Elvis was already fat.

Jane Wagner

Is there some principle of nature which states that we never know the quality of what we have until it is gone?

Richard Hofstadter

Relationships

Women and men . . . men and women. It will never work.

Erica Jong

It's one thing to tolerate a boring marriage; a boring affair does *not* make sense.

Jane Wagner

Relationships that do not end peacefully, do not end at all.

Merrit Malloy

The lion and the calf shall lie down together, but the calf won't get much sleep.

Woody Allen

The easiest kind of relationship for me is with ten thousand people. The hardest is with one.

Joan Baez

The trouble with loving is that pets don't last long enough and people last too long.

Unknown

The one who loves the least controls the relationship.

Dr. Robert Anthony

Men learn to love the women they are attracted to and women become attracted to the men they love.

Sex, Lies & Videotape

I will not be ignored.

Fatal Attraction

I told you 158 times I cannot stand little notes on my pillow. "We are out of cornflakes. F.U." It took me three hours to figure out F.U. was Felix Ungar. It's not your fault, Felix; it's a rotten combination.

Oscar Madison, *The Odd Couple*

The difference between men friends and women friends is that men tend to do things together, women tend just to be together.

Art Jahnke

Carmine and I have an understanding. I'm allowed to date other men, and he's allowed to date ugly women.

"Laverne & Shirley"

Y'know, when we're not fighting, we get along just fine.

"Rockford Files"

If you don't think women are explosive, drop one.

Gerald F. Lieberman

I was just inches from a clean getaway.

Jack Nicholson to
Shirley MacLaine,
Terms of Endearment

Once the trust goes out of a relationship, it's really no fun lying to 'em anymore.

Norm Peterson, "Cheers'

A relationship is what happens when two people are waiting for something better to come along.

Anonymous

There is no greater experience than to be wanted.

Moondog, N.Y. street poet

There are three parties in every relationship. There's the man, there's the woman, and there's the man and the woman together. When the first two break up, the third one is still l?oving.

Artie Butler

Religion

Anybody can be Pope; the proof is that I have become one.

Pope John XXIII

I'm a Scotch Calvinist and nothing makes us happier than misery.

James Reston

Saints are usually killed by their own people.

Eric Sevareid

One man's theology is another man's belly laugh.

Robert Heinlein

Look busy.

Cardinal Spellman
(in response to having been asked for advice when told a man claiming he was Jesus Christ was at the front door)

Every day people are straying away from the church and going back to God.

Lenny Bruce

If I'm going to hell, I'm going there playing the piano.

Jerry Lee Lewis

Converts are the worst kind of bigots.

Edison Carter, "Max Headroom"

Going to church doesn't make you a Christian any more than going to a garage makes you a car.

Laurence J. Peter

Every religion, every mythology is true in this sense: It is true as metaphorical of the human and cosmic mystery.

Joseph Campbell

A person who says "I'm enlightened," probably isn't.

Baba Ram Dass

In some ways, religion is to spirituality as ideology is to thought.

Arnold Rampersad

Revelations

Some of us are becoming the men we wanted to marry.
                                        Gloria Steinem

There is no such thing as a self-cleaning oven.
                                        Wes Smith

Deep down, I'm pretty superficial.
                                        Ava Gardner

They're ba-ack!
                    Heather O'Rourke, *Poltergeist II*

Time has little to do with infinity or jelly doughnuts.
                    Thomas Magnum, "Magnum P.I."

That old law about "an eye for an eye" leaves every-body blind.
                                        Martin Luther King, Jr.

Many are called; but few are called back
                                        Sister Mary Tricky

Revolution

Revolution is a trivial shift in the emphasis of suffering.
Tom Stoppard

In perpetrating a revolution, there are two require-
ments: someone or something to revolt against and
someone to actually show up and do the revolting.
Dress is usually casual.
Woody Allen

A revolution is interesting insofar as it avoids like the
plague the plague it promises to heal.
Daniel Berrigan

I was probably the only revolutionary ever referred to as
"cute".
Abbie Hoffman

Every successful revolution puts on in time the robe of
the tyrant it has deposed.
Barbara Tuchman

The Rich

If God hadn't meant for there to be poor people, He wouldn't have given you all their money.

> Revivalist minister addressing
> wealthy congregation, "SCTV"

The rich have a passion for bargains as lively as it is pointless.

> Francoise Sagan

I have no problem with the rich, only with those who have a problem being rich.

> David Brown

Rich people are just poor people with money.

> Sister Mary Tricky

Risk

There's no such thing as a sure thing. That's why they call it gambling.

Oscar Madison, "The Odd Couple"

To be on the wire is life—the rest is waiting.

Roy Scheider to his angel of death,
All That Jazz

If you choose to live outside the law, you must obey the law more stringently than anyone.

Bob Dylan

In order to find the edge, you must risk going over the edge.

Dennis Dugan

You can't expect to hit the jackpot if you don't put a few nickels in the machine.

Flip Wilson

How far is far, how high is high?
We'll never know until we try.

From the California Special Olympics song

Romance

In a great romance, each person basically plays a part that the other really likes.

Elizabeth Ashley

Bisexuality immediately doubles your chances for a date on Saturday night.

Woody Allen

The piano bar is the gateway to the halls of masturbation.

Henry Miller

Never confuse "I love you" with "I want to marry you."

Leroy King

247

Rules, Laws, & Theorems

People who stare each other in the eye for sixty seconds straight will soon either be fighting or making love.

Peter Butler

Nothing is ever accomplished by a reasonable man.

Bucy's Law

A home is ruled by the sickest person in it.

Nitzberg's Observation

Poverty is life's cheapest lesson.

Form's Facts

If you have to learn it from a self-help book, you may be beyond help.

Wes Smith

Flattery is the sincerest form of lying.

Bradley's rules

Soderquist's Paradox: There are more horses' asses than horses.

John Peers

The volume of paper expands to fill the available briefcases.

Jerry Brown

The roe is reputed to sleep for a thousand years and then suddenly rise in flames, particularly if it was smoking when it dozed off.

Woody Allen

You gotta know the rules before you can break em'. Otherwise, it's just no fun.

Sonny Crockett, "Miami Vice"

Claustrophobia? It's a dreadful fear of Santa Claus.

Vinnie Barbarino, "Welcome Back Kotter"

As we say in the sewer, time and tide wait for no man.

Ed Norton, "The Honeymooners"

A psychotic thinks that 2 plus 2 makes 5. A neurotic KNOWS that 2 plus 2 makes 4—he just can't stand it.

'80s Anonymous

McGinn's Law: Just about everything takes longer than they say it does, except sex.

Jim McGinn

The human brain starts working the moment you are born and never stops until you stand up to speak in public.

George Jessel

The law of raspberry jam: The wider any culture is spread, the thinner it gets.

Alvin Toffler

Salutations

May the force be with you.

George Lucas

May the Schwartz be with you.

Mel Brooks

Here's looking at you kid.

Humphrey Bogart as Rick, *Casablanca*

For the audience, without whom I would only be
 myself.

Steve Martin

My name is Bond—James Bond.

Sean Connery, *James Bond*

Goo-od Morning, Vietnam!

Robin Williams, in
Good Morning, Vietnam

San Francisco

San Francisco is like granola: Take away the fruits and nuts, and all you have are the flakes.

Unknown

In San Francisco, Halloween is redundant.

Will Durst

Science

Most "scientists" are bottlewashers and button sorters.

Robert Heinlein

If I had as many affairs as they say, I would now be speaking to you from inside a jar at the Harvard Medical School.

Frank Sinatra

Certain things in our universe are fixed and absolute. The sun always rises in the east. Parking meters are always set to give an edge to the meter maid. And sons never phone.

Brian Devlin, "The Devlin Connection"

The laws of biology are the fundamental lessons of history.

Will and Ariel Durant

Screenwriting

A dramatic writer should never tell anything he can show.

Nunnally Johnson

If all that's going on in your scenes is what's going on in your scenes, think about it a long time.

William Goldman

I don't write pictures about tomatos that eat people. I write pictures about people who eat tomatos.

Julie Epstein

A screenplay is a story told with pictures.

Syd Field

Whatever you do in terms of telling a story, the most important thing that you can define is who you are.

John Patrick Shanley

Security

Security is a kind of death.

Tennessee Williams

I have an intense desire to return to the womb. Anybody's.

Woody Allen

Serenity

God grant me the serenity
to accept the things I cannot change.
Courage to change the things I can
and Wisdom to know the difference.

The Serenity Prayer, A.A.

If you want serenity, try not to yell about it.

Mary's Almanac

Sex

Is sex dirty? Only if it's done right.

Woody Allen

Everybody lies about sex.

Robert Heinlein

If I have to cry, I think of my sex life. If I have to laugh, I think of my sex life.

Glenda Jackson

A promiscuous person is someone who is getting more sex than you are.

Victor Lownes

Sex should be friendly. Otherwise stick to mechanical toys; it's more sanitary.

Robert Heinlein

Sex is the most fun you can have without a gun.

Ernestyne White

To me the term "sexual freedom" meant freedom from having to have sex.

Jane Wagner

A hard man is good to find.

Mae West

You sleep with a guy once and before you know it he wants to take you to dinner.

Myers Yori

In America, sex is an obsession; in other parts of the world it is a fact.

Marlene Dietrich

All cats are not gray after midnight.

Robert Heinlein

Two is company; three is fifty bucks.

Joan Rivers

The reason people sweat is so they don't catch fire when making love.

Don Rose

It's been so long since I made love, I can't even remember who gets tied up.

Joan Rivers

Sex is good, but not as good as fresh sweet corn.

Garrison Keillor

People don't need sex so much as they need to be listened to.

Jane Wagner

What I like about masturbation is that you don't have to talk afterwards.

Milos Forman

You must force sex to do the work of love and love to do the work of sex.

Mary McCarthy

A eunuch is a man who has had his work cut out for him.

Robert Burns

Power is the ultimate aphrodisiac.

Henry Kissinger

If God had meant for us to have group sex, he'd have given us more organs.

Malcolm Bradbury

I mean, what good is it, Sis, to have sexual freedom if you become a slave to it.

Jane Wagner

A kiss is a lovely trick designed by nature to stop speech when words become superfluous.

Ingrid Bergman

A satisfying sex life is the single most effective protection against heart attacks.

Dr. Eugene Scheimann

When turkeys mate they think of swans.

Johnny Carson

Sex is the biggest nothing of all time.

Andy Warhol

The good thing about masturbation is that you don't have to dress up for it.

Truman Capote

Last time I made love to my wife nothing was happening, so I said to her, "What's the matter? You can't think of anybody either?"

Rodney Dangerfield

Sex is like supermarkets: overrated . . . a lot of pushing and shoving and you still come out with very little in the end.

Shirley Valentine

Peggy, you know what a penis is—stay away from it.
Barbara Harris to Kathleen Turner,
Peggy Sue Got Married

I make it a policy never to have sex before the first date.

Sally Field to Michael Caine, *Surrender*

Sex is the most fun you can have without smiling.

> Madonna

My shorts have more ambition than I do.

> Alex Reiger, "Taxi"

The real fountain of youth is to have a dirty mind.

> Jerry Hall

You American girls have such big breasts all the time. So, please give us the number of your apartment so we can go up there and have sex with you NOW!

> Steve Martin as "The Wild 'n' Crazy Guy,"
> "Saturday Night Live"

Come on, Chawley. Ya wanna do it? Let's do it, right here on the Oriental.

> Angelica Huston,
> *Prizzi's Honor*

Mother, you who conceived without sinning, teach me how to sin without conceiving.

> Katia Yaksic

Do not have sex with people that you do not know and whose state you cannot attest to.

> Surgeon General C. Everett Coop

The difference between pornography and erotica is lighting.

> Gloria Leonard

Think of me as a sex symbol for the men who don't give a damn.

Phyllis Diller

The only people who make love all the time are liars.

Telly Savalas

Pornography tells lies about women. But pornography tells the truth about men.

John Stoltenberg

This is the damndest season I ever seen: the Durham Bulls can't lose and I can't get laid.

Susan Sarandon, *Bull Durham*

Show Business

Whom God wishes to destroy, He first makes successful in show business.

Francis Coppola

Only at a wrap party will you find Hitler dancing with a dolly grip.

Lee Philips

If you can tune into the fantasy life of an eleven-year-old girl, you can make a fortune in this business.

George Lucas

Changing agents is like changing deck chairs on the *Titanic*.

Judy Thomas

Here the phony tinsel is stripped away and you can see the real tinsel.

Mike Romanoff, on his restaurant

Signature Lines

Don't have a cow, man.

Bart Simpson

Live from New York, it's Saturday night!

SNL Opening

I have a dream.

Martin Luther King

We'll be right back.

Johnny Carson

Who loves ya, baby?

Telly Savalas

Let's get busy.

Arsenio Hall

Isn't that *special?*

Dana Carvey as the Church Lady,
"Saturday Night Live"

I'm outa here.

> Dennis Miller, "Saturday Night Live"

Here's Johnny!

> Ed McMahon

Free at last! Free at last!

> Martin Luther King

Trust me.

> Joe Izuzu

Ttthat's all, folks.

> Porky Pig

And that's the way it is.

> Walter Cronkite

Underachiever. . . and proud of it.

> Bart Simpson

Float like a butterfly, sting like a bee.

> Muhammad Ali

Yaba-daba-doo.

> Fred Flintstone

What's up, Doc?

> Bugs Bunny

Stifle yourself, Edith.

Archie Bunker, "All in the Family"

Slogans

I am not a bimbo!

> Jessica Hahn

Just say no.

> '80s Anti-Drug Slogan

Know when to say when.

> Spuds MacKenzie

I live for the moment to hit people.

> Mike Tyson

I like Ike.

> Eisenhower campaign slogan

I'm OK, You're OK.

> Eric Berne

Let go and let God.

Alcoholics Anonymous

If I can make it, you can make it.

Rev. Jesse Jackson

Quality is Job 1.

Ad for Ford Motors

Build your future on the rock.

The Prudential Insurance Co.

It takes a big airline to make a small world.

Ad for KLM

Why follow the crowd when you can draw one of your own?

Ad for Lotus motor cars

One day at a time.

Alcoholics Anonymous

Enquiring minds want to know.

Motto, *National Enquirer*

For the woman who wasn't born yesterday.

Motto, *Lear's* magazine

Be all that you can be.

U.S. Army Slogan

Now that I'm gone, I tell you: don't smoke, whatever you do, don't smoke.

> Yul Brynner, cancer victim in a
> posthumous anti-smoking commercial

Easy does it.

> Alcoholics Anonymous

Live and let live.

> Alanon

Please don't squeeze the Charmin.

> Mr. Whipple, Ad for Charmin

The success hasn't gone to our price.

> Ad for Peugeot

Get Met—it pays.

> Ad for Metropolitan Life Insurance Co.

Space

Why do we always expect them to come in metal ships?
Invasion of the Body Snatchers

This is one small step for a man, one giant leap for mankind.

Neil Armstrong (as he became the first man to set foot on the moon)

Space is really big—REALLY big.

Douglas Adams, *The Hitchhiker's Guide to the Universe*

The eagle has landed.

Neil Armstrong

I suppose the one quality in astronauts more powerful than any other is curiosity. They have to get some place nobody's ever been before.

John Glenn

Spirituality

Pressed, I would define spirituality as the shadow of light humanity casts as it moves through the darkness of everything that can't be explained.

John Updike

Spirituality is as much an ability to accept love as it is a capacity for loving.

Francine du Plessix Gray

The spiritual life becomes very simple when you're sick.

Wilfrid Sheed

Spirituality is a kind of virgin wisdom, a knowing that comes prior to experience.

Marilyn Ferguson

We deny the existence of spirit and then are helpless before it's raw power. We talk much about it, then refuse to live as though it really matters.

Arnold Rampersad

Sports

A tie game is like kissing your sister.

> J.C. Humes

If the people don't want to come out to the park, nobody's gonna stop them.

> Yogi Berra

There are more pleasant things to do than beat up people.

> Muhammad Ali

If Shakespeare had been in pro basketball, he never would have had time to write his soliloquies. He would have always been on a plane between Phoenix and Kansas City.

> Paul Westhead,
> Basketball coach

He had a God-given killer instinct.

> Al Davis of the Oakland
> Raiders, on George Blanda

I never met a man I didn't want to fight.

> Pro Football Lineman
> Lyle Alzado

I'm no different from anybody else with two arms, two legs, and forty-two hundred hits.

> Pete Rose

Golf is a game with the soul of a 1954 Rotarian.

> Bill Mandel

If I ever needed a brain transplant, I'd choose a sportswriter because I'd want a brain that had never been used.

> Norm Van Brocklin

Very few blacks will take up golf until the requirement for plaid pants is dropped.

> Franklyn Ajaye

Football players, like prostitutes, are in the business of ruining their bodies for the pleasure of strangers.

> Merle Kessler

A team should be an extension of the coach's personality. My teams are arrogant and obnoxious.

> Al McGuire, former
> basketball coach

Nolan Ryan is pitching a lot better now that he has his curve ball straightened out.

> Joe Garagiola

Winning is not everything. It's the only thing.

Vince Lombardi

My toughest fight was with my first wife.

Muhammad Ali

Tennis is like marrying for money. Love has nothing to
do with it.

Phyllis Diller

I never bet on baseball.

Pete Rose

You've got to take the initiative and play your game. In
a decisive set, confidence is the difference.

Chris Evert

If you want to meet new people, pick up the wrong golf
ball.

Anonymous

Boxing is rough. Even if you win, you get hurt.

Joyce Carol Oates

Drive for show. But putt for dough.

Bobby Locke

Kill the body and the head will die.

Smokin' Joe Frazier

When you get on first, know you are going to second. Know you can beat the pitcher and the catcher and the two of them combined. You have to have an inner conceit to be a successful base stealer. You have to know you are better than either the pitcher or the catcher.

Pete Reiser to Maury Wills

Like my old skeenball coach used to say, "Find out what you don't do well, then don't do it."

"Alf"

Baseball is like church. Many attend. Few understand.

Leo Durocher

I could have played football for two or three more years. All I needed was a leg transplant.

John Unitas

Thinking . . . is what gets you caught from behind.

O.J. Simpson

How can you think and hit at the same time?

Yogi Berra

I don't think we can win every game. Just the next one.

Lou Holtz

No one man is superior to the game.

A. Bartlett Giammatti

Strategy

Whatever you think it's gonna take, double it. That applies to money, time, stress. It's gonna be harder than you think and take longer than you think.

Richard A. Cortese (on
starting your own business)

The eleventh commandment of a motion picture nego-
tiation: Thou shalt not take less than thy last deal.

John Gregory Dunne

The trick is to avoid the pitfalls, seize the opportunities, and get back home by six o'clock.

Woody Allen, "My Speech to
the Graduates"

Style

Joan of Arc had style. Jesus had style.

Charles Bukowski

Style is primarily a matter of instinct.

Bill Blass

A magazine to have style, must need and understand and invest in what jingles — not jiggles — in designer jeans.

Frances Lear

Fashions fade, style is eternal.

Yves St. Laurent

Success

I don't know the key to success, but the key to failure is trying to please everybody.

Bill Cosby

Nothing like the appearance of success, succeeds.

Christopher Lascl

Oddly enough, success over a period of time is more expensive than failure.

Grant Tinker

I'd like to be lucky enough so that I could throw the soap away after the letters are worn off.

Andy Rooney

It's not that I'm not grateful for all this attention. It's just that fame and fortune ought to add up to more than fame and fortune.

Robert Fulghum

Taxes

Taxes are not levied for the benefit of the taxed.

Robert Heinlein

The rich aren't like us; they pay less taxes.

Peter De Vries

The wages of sin are unreported.

Anonymous

Suppose we had to pay taxes on what we think we're worth?

Anonymous

Income taxes are the most imaginative fiction written today.

Herman Wouk

Only little people pay taxes.

Leona Helmsley

Technology

Computers are useless. They can only give you answers.

Pablo Picasso

The computer is down. I hope it's something serious.

Stanton Delaplane

I have a microwave fireplace. You can lay down in front of the fire all night in eight minutes.

Stephen Wright

Chrome wasn't built in a day.

Aesop, Jr., "The Bullwinkle Show"

For tribal man space was the uncontrollable mystery. For technological man it is time that occupies the same role.

Marshall McLuhan

Television

Television is an invention that permits you to be entertained in your living room by people you wouldn't have in your home.

David Frost

Television is democracy at its ugliest.

Paddy Chayefsky

If it wasn't for Philo T. Farnsworth, inventor of television, we'd still be eating frozen radio dinners.

Johnny Carson

Television has proved that people will look at anything rather than each other.

Ann Landers

When I was young we didn't have MTV. We had to take drugs and go to concerts.

Steven Pearl

Television deprives children of their imaginations.

Theodore Isaac Rubin, M.D.

No wonder they call television a medium; it's so seldom rare and well-done.

Mighty Mouse

Television has done much for psychiatry by spreading information about it, as well as contributing to the need for it.

Alfred Hitchcock

In our business, morals are one thing, but ratings are everything.

Max Headroom, "Max Headroom"

Dealing with network executives is like being nibbled to death by ducks.

Eric Sevaraid, CBS News

I was cable when cable wasn't cool.

Ted Turner

The medium is the message.

Marshall McLuhan

The principal contributor to loneliness in this country is television. What happens is that the family "gets together" alone.

Ashley Montagu, Ph.D.

Time

Infinity, it could be time on an ego trip for all I know.

Jane Wagner

A man with one watch knows what time it is. A man who two watches is never sure.

John Peer

There is never enough time, unless you're serving it.

Malcolm Forbes

The future is much like the present, only longer.

Don Quisenberry

Time is truly the great enemy. It's not the great healer, it's the great stealer.

Sylvester Stallone

There's no present. There's only the immediate future and the recent past.

George Carlin

It's hard to believe a half hour has gone by when it only feels like thirty minutes.

Kelly Monteith, "Hit Squad"

Timing

The trick is to be there when it's settled.

Arthur Goldberg

What a gigantic step it is not to move.

Merrit Malloy

Hurry? I have no time to hurry.

Igor Stravinsky

You mean they've scheduled Yom Kippur opposite "Charlie's Angels"?

Fred Silverman

If you're not beguiling by age twelve, forget it.

Lucy to Charlie Brown

You shouldn't blow the chance when you've got the chance to say . . . "I love you . . . I honestly love you."

Song by Peter Allen

You have to think about one shot. One shot is what it's all about. The deer has to be taken with one shot. I try to tell people that — they don't listen.

Robert DeNiro, *The Deer Hunter*

When you find the person you want to spend the rest of your life with, you want the rest of your life to begin as soon as possible.

Billy Crystal, *When Harry Met Sally*

Don't wait for your "ship to come in," and feel angry and cheated when it doesn't. Get going with something small.

Dr. Irene Kassorla

You never get a second chance to make a first impression.

Head and Shoulders Commercial

There's time to be Daniel Boone, and there's time to be a plumber.

"MacGyver"

If it's going to come out eventually, better it come out immediately.

Henry Kissinger

I am minutes ahead of my time.

Lotus Weinstock

Isn't it just like Jesus to be born on Christmas morning?

Mary's Almanac

The word "now" is like a bomb through the window, and it ticks.

Arthur Miller

Trust

Trust is doing something someone asks you to do, even
if you think it's dumb.

Starman

Trust is an extra arm.

Sister Mary Tricky

Truth

The truth is the safest lie.

Anonymous

If you're going to tell people the truth, be funny or they'll kill you.

Billy Wilder

The truth of a proposition has nothing to do with its credibility. And vice versa.

Robert Heinlein

I never know how much of what I say is true.

Bette Midler

The truth isn't what we say, it's how we feel when we say it.

Merrit Malloy

It must be Sunday, everybody's telling the truth.

Song lyric, sung by Phoebe Snow

A woman does not break into your house and clean it for fun.

> Rick Simon, "Simon & Simon"

I told 'em the truth and they fell for it.

> Judge Harry Stone,
> "Night Court"

That's not a lie, it's a terminological inexactitude.

> Alexander Haig,
> 1983 TV news interview

Desperation tends to make one flexible.

> "MacGyver"

When all else fails, tell the truth.

> Line quoted by Donald T. Regan

Always tell the truth. It's the world's best lie.

> Uncle Martin, "My Favorite Martian"

One Cardinal Rule: One must always listen to the patient.

> Dr. Oliver Sacks

Truth may be stranger than fiction, but fiction is truer.

> Anonymous

The more you try to avoid suffering, the more you suffer because smaller things begin to torture you in proportion to your fear of suffering.

> Thomas Merton

Searching for simple answers rarely uncovers the truth. Instead, it leads to superstition, prejudice, panic and war.

K.C. Cole

I searched through rebellion, drugs, diet, mysticism, religion, intellectualism and much more, only to begin to find that truth is basically simple and feels good, clear and right.

Chick Corea

There's an element of truth in every idea that lasts long enough to be called corny.

Irving Berlin

T-Shirt Slogans

It's never too late to have a happy childhood.

Get even. Live long enough to be a problem to your kids.

Don't start with me. You know how I get.

Life is a bitch. Then you die. Have a nice day.

Don't tell me what kind of day to have.

If you don't like the way I drive, get off the sidewalk.

If you love someone, set them free. If they don't come back, hunt them down and shoot them.

Don't drink and drive. You may hit a bump and spill your drink.

Trust me. I'm a doctor.

So many men, so little time.

Stress—that confusion created when the mind must override the body's basic desire to choke the living crap out of some idiot who desperately needs it.

Lawyer: Individual whose principal role is to protect his clients from other members of his profession.

Old sailors never die, they just get a little dinghy.

Tease me about my age and I'll beat you with my cane.

Marines never die, they just go to hell and regroup.

Fishermen have great rods.

Engineers know all the angles.

My other body is in the shop.

Of all the things I've lost, the thing I miss the most is my mind.

No mother, I haven't met Mr. Right yet . . . but I have met Mr. Cheap, Mr. Rude, and Mr. Married.

I feel like such a failure. I've been shopping for over twenty years and I still have nothing to wear.

Vanity

You're so vain, you probably think this song is about you.

Song lyric, Carly Simon

I'll destroy you. I am the master of disaster.

Muhammad Ali

If you have to tell them who you are, you aren't anybody.

Gregory Peck

Enough about me. Now, let's talk about you. Tell me. What do you think about me?

Anonymous

I have my faults, but being wrong ain't one of them.

Jimmy Hoffa

If you look good and dress well, you don't need a purpose in life.

Robert Pante
Fashion Consultant

It matters not whether you win or lose; what matters is
whether I win or lose.

Darren Winberg

I guess I'm larger than life. That's my problem.

Bette Davis

You can say I'm full of shit, but don't say I'm old.

Zsa Zsa Gabor

Violence

Cigarettes can kill, but so can love, and so can Lola.
>Lola Heatherton, "SCTV"

Never settle with words what you can accomplish with a flamethrower.
>Bruce Feirstein

Vision

We shall overcome.

Civil Rights slogan

You have to believe in gods to see them.

Hopi the Indian, "Gumby"

When I was dead I saw God. She looks like Toody from "The Facts of Life."

Larry, "Newhart"

Remembering and seeing are not the same, and that is why memories are of little use to us in forming loving relationships.

Gerald Jampolsky

Nobody sees anybody truly but only through the flaws of their own ego.

Tennessee Williams

War & Peace

Our ultimate strength is an eternal idea, not a gun.

Terry Sanford

You can have peace. Or you can have freedom. Don't ever count on having both at once.

Robert Heinlein

If it's natural to kill, why do men have to go into training to learn how?

Joan Baez

Peace is an extension of war by political means.

Robert Heinlein

If you want peace, understand war.

B.H. Lidell Hart (as quoted by Richard Nixon)

Go to war. Keep the world safe for hypocrisy.

"Laugh-In"

I took a speed reading course and I read *War and Peace.* It involves Russia.

Woody Allen

We do not consider it an acceptable cease-fire when we cease and the Contras fire.

Daniel Ortega

The causes of war are the same as the causes of competition among individuals: acquisitiveness, pugnacity, and pride; the desire for food, land, materials, fuels, mastery.

Will and Ariel Durant

War is the biggest ego trip of all time.

Molly Wiest

Winning & Losing

Nice guys finish last.

Leo Durocher

Who said nice guys finish last?

George Bush
(upon winning Illinois primary)

Every time a friend succeeds, I die a little.

Gore Vidal

You always pass failure on the way to success.

Mickey Rooney

Fear of losing is what makes competitors so great. Show me a gracious loser and I'll show you a permanent loser.

O.J. Simpson

Wisdom

Whosoever loveth wisdom is righteous, but he that keepeth company with fowl is weird.

Woody Allen

Be happy. It is a way of being wise.

Colette

The quieter you become, the more you can hear.

Baba Ram Dass

A truly wise man never plays leapfrog with a unicorn.

"Banacek"

If you can't say anything — don't.

Hilaire Tattinger

Let me tell you girls the three most important things I learned about life. Number one: Hold fast to your friends. Number two: There's no such thing as security. Number three: Don't go see *Ishtar*.

Sophia, "The Golden Girls"

Swallow what's bitter in the cup and move on.

Howard Hunter, "Hill Street Blues"

If you can't tie good knots, tie plenty of them.

Yachtsmen's credo

Follow the rules of holes: If you are in one, stop digging.

Dennis Healy

It's necessary to be slightly underemployed if you are to do something significant.

James Watson, Nobel Laureate

If you're old, don't try to change yourself, change your environment.

B.F. Skinner

Only a fool fights in a burning house.

Kang, "Star Trek"

You can't be depressed and grateful at the same time.

Randall Miller, trombone player

The only Zen you find on the top of mountains is the Zen you bring up there.

Robert Persig

When one door of happiness closes, another opens; but often we look so long at the closed door that we do not see the one which has been opened for us.

Helen Keller

There are some people that if they don't know, you can't tell 'em.

Louis Armstrong

Discipline does not mean suppression or control, nor is it adjustment to a pattern of ideology. It means a mind that sees "what is" and learns "what was."

Krishnamurti

When our knowledge coalesces with our humanity and our humor, it can add up to wisdom.

Carol Orlock

Things don't change. You change your way of looking, that's all.

Carlos Castaneda

Women

I don't know why women want any of the things that men have when one of the things that women have is men.

Coco Chanel

A woman without a man is like a fish without a bicycle.

Gloria Steinem

There's a great woman behind every idiot.

John Lennon

Being a woman is of special interest to aspiring male transsexuals. To actual women it is simply a good excuse not to play football.

Fran Liebowitz

You don't know anything about a woman until you meet her in court.

Norman Mailer

The trouble with some women is that they get all excited about nothing and then marry him.

Cher

Plain women know more about men than beautiful ones do.

Katharine Hepburn

Women, can't live with them, can't shoot them.

Stephen Wright

There's no getting around it. Women cost money.

Bud Anderson,
"Father Knows Best"

It's not the frivolity of women that makes them so intolerable. It's their ghastly enthusiasm.

Horace Rumpole,
"Rumpole of the Bailey"

You know women—they hear goodbye in your voice and their lower lip starts trembling. The next thing you know you're buying them something fuel-injected.

Charles Kincaid, "Double
Trouble"

Women are never what they seem to be. There is the woman you see and the woman who is hidden. Buy the gift for the woman who is hidden.

Erma Bombeck

The more independent you want to be, the more generous you must be with yourself as a woman.

Diane Von Furstenberg

To be one woman, truly, wholly, is to be all women.
Tend one garden and you will birth worlds.

Kate Braverman

Women are the most powerful magnet in the universe;
all men are cheap metal.

Larry Miller

The Rose Bowl is the only one I've ever seen that I
didn't have to clean.

Erma Bombeck

One of these days, Alice, right to the moon!
Ralph Kramden, "The Honeymooners"

Whatever women do, they must do twice as well as men
to be thought half as good. Luckily, this is not
difficult.

Charlotte Whitton

Work

No matter what you do, do your best at it. If you're going to be a bum, be the best bum there is.

Robert Mitchum

If you aren't fired with enthusiasm, you will be fired with enthusiasm.

Vince Lombardi

You have to take your job seriously, but you can't take yourself seriously.

Brent Mussburger

Customers give carpenters the hardest time on the smallest jobs.

Antonio Farilla, carpenter

The secret of a long life is double careers. One to about age 60, then another for the next thirty years.

David Ogilvy

Don't stay in bed . . . unless you make money in bed.

George Burns

No matter who you are or what you plan to do, learn to type.

Liz Smith

The harder you work, the luckier you get.

Gary Player

Work is difficult; that's why it's called work.

David Brown

Writers

In six pages, I can't even say "Hello."

James Michener

Writers talk too much.

Lillian Hellman

First coffee. Then a bowel movement. Then the muse joins me.

Gore Vidal

Writers should be read — but neither seen nor heard.

Daphne Du Maurier

The first thing to look out for after your first big success are drugs and screenplays.

Richard Price

Writing

I want to pay tribute to my four writers: Matthew, Mark, Luke and John.

> Bishop Fulton Sheen

A poet who reads his verse in public may have other nasty habits.

> Robert Heinlein

The role of a writer is not to say what we all can say but what we are unable to say.

> Anais Nin

A new regulation for the publishing industry: "The advance for a book must be larger than the check for the lunch at which it was discussed."

> Calvin Trillin

If you want privacy, don't sleep with a writer.

> Marilyn Peterson

Don't ever tell a story like it wasn't about you.

> Merrit Malloy

I shall live badly if I do not write, and I shall write badly if I do not live.

Francoise Sagan

Writing is turning one's worst moments into money.

J.P. Donleavy

I write fiction because it is a way of making statements I can disown, and I write plays because dialogue is the most respectable way of contradicting myself.

Tom Stoppard

Originality is the science of concealing your sources.

Unknown

Finishing a book is just like you took a child out in the back yard and shot it.

Truman Capote

I'm working when I'm fighting with my wife. I constantly ask myself—how can I use this stuff to literary advantage.

Art Buchwald

Never let a domestic quarrel ruin a day's writing. If you can't start the next day fresh, get rid of your wife.

Mario Puzo

Whenever I'm asked what kind of writing is the most lucrative, I have to say, ransom notes.

H.N. Swanson
Literary Agent

Writing is the hardest way of earning a living, with the possible exception of wrestling alligators.

Olin Miller

A writer should concern himself with whatever absorbs his fancy, stirs his heart, and unlimbers his type-writer. . . . A writer has the duty to be good, not lousy: true, not false; lively, not dull; accurate, not full of error. He should tend to lift people up, not lower them down.

E.B. White

The great thing about writing: Stay with it . . . ultimately you teach yourself something very important about yourself.

Bernard Malamud

If you want to "get in touch with your feelings," fine, talk to yourself. We all do. But if you want to communicate with another thinking human being, get in touch with your thoughts. Put them in order, give them a purpose, use them to persuade, to instruct, to discover, to seduce. The secret way to do this is to write it down, and then cut out the confusing parts.

William Safire

The thing that usually gets me through the writing is that my feelings of wretched inadequacy are irregularly punctuated by brief flashes of omnipotence.

James L. Brooks

Have faith. May you surround yourself with parents, editors, mates and children as tolerant and supportive as mine have been. But the essential support and encouragement of course comes from within, arising out of the mad notion that your society needs to know what only you can tell it.

John Updike

Find a subject you care about and which you in your heart feel others should care about. It is the genuine caring, and not your games with language, which will be the most compelling and seductive element in your style.

Kurt Vonnegut

Words, as is well known, are great foes of reality.

Joseph Conrad

Painting and potting are crafts. Writing is an addiction.

Jim McGinn

Youth

People think that I'm tough and strong and that I kicked my way through everything. But they are wrong. The truth is that when I was young I was adorable and a trembling wreck.

Katharine Hepburn

I like young girls. Their stories are shorter.

Tom McGuane

Gangs are a group reaction to helplessness.

Rev. Jesse Jackson

There's nothing worse than being an aging young person.

Richard Pryor

The young always have the same problem — how to rebel and conform at the same time. They have solved this by defying their parents and copying one another.

Quentin Crisp

Intensity is so much more becoming in the young.

Joanne Woodward

Index Notes

ABOUT THE AUTHORS

Merrit Malloy and Shauna Sorensen both live and work in Los Angeles. This book is the happy result of their seventeen-year friendship, which includes a partnership in several professional and literary endeavors.*

Shauna Sorensen is a former editor-in-chief of a publishing house and has owned her own literary agency. She has written numerous articles for newspapers and magazines, including *Architectural Digest, New West*, and *Los Angeles* magazine. She has a degree in law and is currently a businesswoman in Los Angeles.

Merrit Malloy is a well known poet and author whose best-selling books include *My Song for Him Who Never Sang to Me, Things I Meant to Say to You When We Were Old, Beware of Older Men, We Hardly See Each Other Anymore*, and *The People Who Couldn't Say Goodbye.*

She is currently at work on her newest book entitled *Winter on a Summer Island*, due out next spring.

*The authors sincerely hope you have as much fun reading through this book as they had putting it together. And they request that if you have any "Quotable Quotes" from your own personal experience, or know of any "gems" that might be included in a further edition, please send all quotes plus source to:

THE QUOTABLE QUOTE BOOK

c/o Pacific Press
2125 Patricia Avenue
Los Angeles, CA 90025